Eyewitness
Baseball

The pitching sequence

Early baseball

Charleston, Arkansas, town team

Umpire

1888 Cincinnati
Reds scorecard

Catcher's glove

Mickey Mantle

Ted Williams's
spikes

Louisville Slugger baseball bat

Eyewitness
Baseball

Written by
JAMES BUCKLEY, JR.

Babe Ruth and Lou Gehrig

2009 Little League World
Series player

Biography of Satchel Paige

Close play at third base

George Brett's
Hall of Fame plaque

DK Publishing

Pitcher

Women's pr[...]
baseball i[...]
the 1940[...]

DK

LONDON, NEW YORK,
MELBOURNE, MUNICH, and DELHI

Editor John Searcy
Publishing Director Beth Sutinis
Designer Jessica Park
Managing Art Editor Michelle Baxter
Production Controller Charlotte Oliver

A Production of the Shoreline Publishing Group
President James Buckley, Jr.
Designer Thomas J. Carling, www.carlingdesign.com
Studio and Memorabilia Photography
Michael Burr and David Spindel

First published in the United States in 2010 by
DK Publishing
375 Hudson Street
New York, New York 10014
10 11 12 13 14 10 9 8 7 6 5 4 3 2 1
176717 – 12/09

DK books are available at special discounts when purchased in bulk
for sales promotions, premiums, fund-raising, or educational use. For
details, contact:

DK Publishing Special Markets
375 Hudson Street
New York, New York 10014
SpecialSales@dk.com

A catalog record for this book is available from the
Library of Congress.

ISBN 978-0-7566-5934-9 (Hardcover)
ISBN 978-0-7566-5935-6 (Library binding)

Color reproduction by Colourscan, Singapore
Printed and bound by Toppan Printing Co.
(Shenzen) Ltd., China

Discover more at
www.dk.com

Bobblehead doll

Player in
1920s
Cleveland
Indians
warm-up
sweater

Hank Aaron

Contents

Base ball beginnings

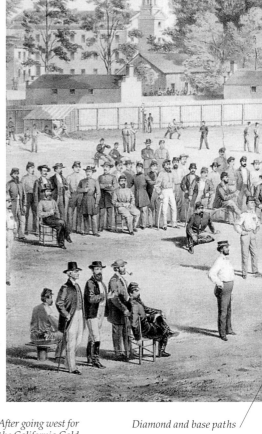

Aℬ BALL, A BAT, AND FOUR BASES ON A FIELD. The elements of the game that became baseball have been around for hundreds of years, most famously in an English game called "rounders." Americans had been playing another ball game with bases called "town ball" since the Revolutionary War. By the 1840s, sportsmen in several northeastern cities were gathering regularly to play several variations of what they called "base ball." In 1845, Alexander Cartwright (inset) and Daniel "Doc" Adams, leaders of the Knickerbocker Base Ball Club, developed the first set of rules for the game. Although those rules changed rapidly over the next few years and continued to evolve into the 1900s, they were close enough to today's rules to mark the "birth" of baseball. Despite humble beginnings, the game has grown from a sport played by gentlemen on weekends to a sport played by men, women, boys, and girls of all ages in more than 100 countries.

After going west for the California Gold Rush of 1849, Cartwright later became a fire chief in Honolulu.

Diamond and base paths

BATTER UP!
From the beginning of the game, baseball bats have maintained their unique shape: thick at the top and tapering to a narrower handle. Early bats did not have as much tapering as today's bats, but their function was the same: "Meet the ball and hit 'em where they ain't."

Thick handle

The author's great-grandfather Nicholas Minden

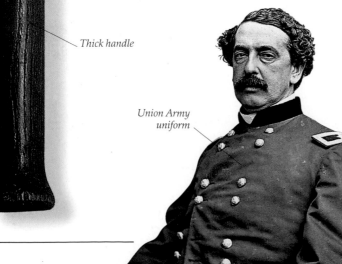

Union Army uniform

THE DOUBLEDAY MYTH
A 1905 commission to trace the "official" origin of baseball somehow settled on the story of Union Army general Abner Doubleday, who, it was claimed, invented the game in 1839 in Cooperstown, New York. Modern research has completely debunked this theory, although the myth of his involvement remains popular today.

TOWN TEAMS
A key to the growth of baseball across America in the late 1800s was the formation of "town teams," such as this one from Charleston, Arkansas (shown before World War I). The players were amateurs, the sponsors local businessmen, and the prize was bragging rights over neighboring towns. But many great players got their start on teams like this one.

Pitcher

Batter

Catcher

BASEBALL HEADS SOUTH
The Civil War (1861–65) helped spread baseball around the country, as Union soldiers took their game, most popular around New York, on the road with them. This noted 1863 lithograph shows Union prisoners at a Confederate camp in Salisbury, North Carolina, putting on a game watched by guards and fellow prisoners alike.

PLAY BALL!
The first baseballs quickly became soft and mushy as play went on. Players soon learned that winding yarn more tightly around a rubber center, then covering it with tightly stitched leather, made a harder ball that traveled farther and lasted longer.

Leather stitching

CASEY AT THE BAT

(This is an excerpt from the most famous baseball poem, written in 1888 by Ernest L. Thayer. It tells the story of a fabled player getting one last chance to save the day.)

Then from 5,000 throats and more there rose a lusty yell;
It rambled through the valley, it rattled in the dell;
It knocked upon the mountain and recoiled upon the flat,
For Casey, mighty Casey, was advancing to the bat….

There was ease in Casey's manner as he stepped into his place;
There was pride in Casey's bearing and a smile on Casey's face.
And when, responding to the cheers, he lightly doffed his hat,
No stranger in the crowd could doubt 'twas Casey at the bat….

[Several stanzas later…]
The sneer is gone from Casey's lip, his teeth are clenched in hate;
He pounds with cruel violence his bat upon the plate.
And now the pitcher holds the ball, and now he lets it go,
And now the air is shattered by the force of Casey's blow.

Oh, somewhere in this favored land the sun is shining bright;
The band is playing somewhere, and somewhere hearts are light,
And somewhere men are laughing, and somewhere children shout;
But there is no joy in Mudville—mighty Casey has struck out.

BASEBALL TUNES
Even bandleader John Philip Sousa (right, in suit) sponsored a team. This song, the "Three Strikes Two-Step," was written in honor of his team. It was one of many tunes, poems (left), and stories about baseball, as it quickly became the "National Pastime."

Birth of the pros

ALTHOUGH BASEBALL'S BEGINNINGS WERE HUMBLE, it didn't take long for players to realize there was a way to make money playing this game. In the years after the Civil War, top players were already being lured from club to club by secret payments. In 1869, the Cincinnati Red Stockings dropped the pretense and announced themselves as professional players. They barnstormed the East, playing (and defeating) all comers. Two years later, the National Association joined together several pro teams to form the first pro league. From then on, baseball would have two worlds: professional and everyone else. In the late 19th century, several pro leagues rose and fell. By 1901, there were two established "major leagues," along with several other "minor" pro leagues, much as there are today.

SPALDING'S SPORT
Albert G. Spalding was a top-notch pitcher in his youth, posting an amazing 55-5 record in 1875. He also helped create the National League in 1876, later became the president of the Chicago White Stockings, and headed a world baseball tour in 1888. In his spare time, he founded the Spalding Sporting Goods Company.

High-button shoes worn for photos, not for games

EARLY CHAMPS
The Baltimore Base Ball Club won the 1894 National League championship. Playing a style of baseball known as "little ball," they were led by the famously fierce player John McGraw.

Championship medal

PRE–WORLD SERIES
The World Series would not begin until 1903, but teams saw the benefit of postseason tournaments early on. From 1894 to 1897, the first- and second-place teams in the National League played each other for the Temple Cup. In 1896 (right), the Baltimore Orioles finished first in the league, and also won the Cup with four straight victories over Cleveland.

EARLY OUTFITS
Early pro players enjoyed snappy outfits as much as today's players do. This heavy wool warm-up sweater was sported by members of the Cleveland Indians, an early entry in the American League.

FOR THE FANS
The growth of pro teams, such as the American Association's Cincinnati Reds (featuring 27-14 pitcher Lee Viau in 1888, below), led to the creation of numerous scorecards, programs, magazines, and souvenirs fans could use to follow their new favorite teams and players.

TAKE ME OUT TO THE BALL GAME

(Written in 1908 by Jack Norworth and Albert Von Tilzer, this song is sung at every baseball game between the top and bottom of the seventh inning—the seventh-inning stretch.)

Take me out to the ball game,
Take me out with the crowd.
Buy me some peanuts and Cracker Jack,
I don't care if I never get back.

Let me root, root, root for the home team.
If they don't win, it's a shame.
For it's one, two, three strikes you're out,
At the old ball game!

Thick ribbed wool

Filed July 5 1869

FIRST NINE OF THE

CINCINNATI
(RED STOCKINGS) BASE BALL CLUB.

Harry Wright

THE FIRST PROS
Harry Wright, captain and founder of the 1869 Cincinnati Red Stockings (left), the first all-professional team, has been called the "father of pro baseball." Along with starting the Red Stockings, Wright invented the basic baseball uniform still used today and patented the first scorecard. He guided his team to an 13-month winning streak, and later led Boston's entry in the new National Association, in 1871.

Note spelling of "Base Ball."

ON THE ROAD
By the turn of the century, Major League baseball had spread as far west as Chicago and St. Louis and as far south as Louisville. This schedule from 1899 also shows the Reds making stops in Washington, Philadelphia, New York, and "Pittsburg," as it was spelled then.

SAFE AT LAST
Early catchers wore little or no safety equipment. Spurred by pro players, the first catcher's masks were developed in the 1870s. This model is from near the turn of the century. It would not be until the years before World War I that catchers regularly began using chest protectors and shin guards.

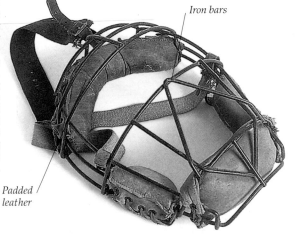

Iron bars

Padded leather

Webbing was a simple leather thong.

Early padded first baseman's glove

GLOVES ON FIRST
First basemen were the first noncatchers to use gloves regularly. Having to catch numerous hard throws throughout a game led to the development of this thickly padded mitt. With its flimsy webbing, it was a far cry from today's big, basketlike gloves.

The Babe

WITHOUT QUESTION, George Herman "Babe" Ruth is the most famous and important baseball player in history. It would be hard to overestimate the impact the Babe had on the game, as both a player and a symbol. His numbers are "Ruthian," a word that today still conjures up both the might of his sweeping swing and his larger-than-life personality. In 22 seasons (1914–35), the Sultan of Swat slugged 714 home runs. To put that in context, the previous career record holder had 138. When Ruth hit 54 home runs for the Yankees in 1920, his total was more than that of most teams, and 25 more than the previous record—set by the Bambino himself in 1919. His best single-season total—60 home runs in 1927—was a record for 34 years. Every home-run hitter—and every world-famous athlete in any sport—competes with the legend of the Babe. It is a battle they can't win.

Ruth used an unusually large 42-ounce (1.2 kg) b...

Officially listed at 215 pounds (98 kg), Ru... often weighed much more.

WHAT MIGHT HAVE BEEN
With Boston from 1914 to 1919, young Babe Ruth was one of baseball's best pitchers. But Red Sox owner Harry Frazee sold Ruth to the New York Yankees in 1919, saddling the Bosox with the "Curse of the Bambino."

A POWERFUL PAIR
Ruth and Lou Gehrig (right) were teammates on the Yankees for 12 years, helping New York win four World Series. Here they are shown in uniforms worn during an off-season exhibition tour. Gehrig was nearly Ruth's equal as a slugger. Sadly, his career was cut short by the illness that now bears his name.

"Larrupin'" was slang for "slugging."

High socks, in the style of the times

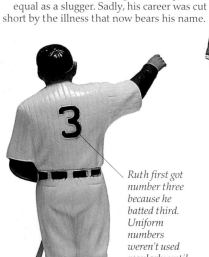

Ruth first got number three because he batted third. Uniform numbers weren't used regularly until the 1930s.

THE "CALLED SHOT"
This statuette of Ruth, showing his famous number 3, recalls one of baseball's most controversial moments. In the 1932 World Series, did Ruth point to the center-field bleachers right before he slugged a homer there? Or was he waving at the Chicago players who were heckling him?

Babe Ruth Pays No Tax On His Size
He Is A Giant in Physique, Still His Royal Clothes Cost Nothing Extra On That Account

AN ADVERTISING BABE
Ruth's incredible popularity allowed him to earn big money (at the time) for endorsements such as this one for large-size men's clothes.

BASEBALL'S MIGHTIEST SWING
Ruth's incredibly quick wrists and powerful upper body helped him hit 714 home runs. But he was more than simply a home-run hitter; Ruth's lifetime batting average of .342 ranks tenth all time.

A baby-faced Ruth got his famous nickname in the minors.

"BABE, SIGN MY BALL"
Some experts believe that Ruth may have signed more autographs than any other sports legend of his day, and certainly more than any today. He signed so many baseballs, bats, programs, and other memorabilia that his signature is not as valuable as other, more reticent stars. He signed this ball the year he died.

BABE ON THE BASE PATHS
Ruth was not the fleetest of runners. In fact, he was thrown out on an attempted steal of second base to end the 1926 World Series. However, his high on-base percentage and outstanding teammates helped him score 2,174 runs (including this one in 1926), tied for fourth-most all-time.

BABE AND HIS BABY
Ruth's daughter Dorothy shared her dad with the kids of the world. Raised in an orphanage, Ruth always had a special place in his heart for his youngest fans.

Umpire using classic outside chest protector and mask.

Both players used Louisville Slugger bats.

RECORD SMASHERS
The bottom bat and ball were used by Ruth to hit his then-record 60th home run in 1927, when he broke his own record of 59. In 1961, Roger Maris of the Yankees broke Ruth's record with his 61st home run, using the bat and ball at the top. Since then, even Maris's total has been topped, first by Mark McGwire's 70 in 1998 and then by Barry Bonds's 73 in 2001.

Player signature burned into wood

THE END
In one of baseball's most memorable and poignant photographs, Babe Ruth bids good-bye to fans at his beloved Yankee Stadium—known throughout its life as "The House that Ruth Built"—weeks before his death from throat cancer in 1948. Using a bat for a cane, he thanked his fans and paid homage to the sport he played like no one else.

Ruth had thin legs and famously small feet for a man his size.

The Major Leagues

THE BEST BASEBALL IN THE WORLD is played by the 30 teams that make up Major League Baseball. The Majors, as it is known, is made of two parts: the 16-team National League (N.L.) and the 14-team American League (A.L.). The N.L. was founded in 1876, while the A.L. started in 1901. The Chicago Cubs survive in their original home from the earliest days of the N.L., while the Boston Red Sox, Chicago White Sox, Cleveland Indians, and Detroit Tigers have always been part of the A.L. Today, Major League teams are found from coast to coast, and even in Canada (home of the Toronto Blue Jays). Major League Baseball runs the All-Star Game, the playoffs, and the World Series, in addition to hiring the umpires and setting the rules for all 30 teams.

FUN FOR THE FANS
While a ball game is a great show on the field, many teams add to the entertainment with promotions, giveaways, and mascots, such as Philadelphia's "Phillie Phanatic" (left). He (or is it "it"?) rides an all-terrain vehicle between innings.

THE ULTIMATE CLOSER
In the Majors today, pitchers (see p.24) have specialized roles. One key member of the lineup is the closer, a pitcher called on to sew up a victory for his team late in the game. This is never more important than in the playoffs and the World Series. And no closer in history has been as successful in those key games as the Yankees' Mariano Rivera. In 29 postseason playoff series, he has eight wins, 39 saves, and a 0.74 ERA.

The Major Leagues

AMERICAN LEAGUE

EAST DIVISION
Baltimore Orioles
Boston Red Sox
New York Yankees
Tampa Bay Rays
Toronto Blue Jays

CENTRAL DIVISION
Chicago White Sox
Cleveland Indians
Detroit Tigers
Kansas City Royals
Minnesota Twins

WEST DIVISION
Los Angeles Angels
Oakland Athletics
Seattle Mariners
Texas Rangers

NATIONAL LEAGUE

EAST DIVISION
Atlanta Braves
Florida Marlins
New York Mets
Philadelphia Phillies
Washington Nationals

CENTRAL DIVISION
Chicago Cubs
Cincinnati Reds
Houston Astros
Milwaukee Brewers
Pittsburgh Pirates
St. Louis Cardinals

WEST DIVISION
Arizona Diamondbacks
Colorado Rockies
Los Angeles Dodgers
San Diego Padres
San Francisco Giants

PRIZE BALL
Record-setting baseballs fly into the stands and become valuable souvenirs. In July 2006, this ball was hit by Barry Bonds of the San Francisco Giants for his 715th career home run, moving him into second-place all-time. It later sold at auction for more than $220,000.

WORLD SUPERSTAR
One of the biggest changes to the Majors in the past decade has been an increase in players from other countries. Seattle outfielder Ichiro Suzuki, a former star in Japan's pro leagues, is one of the best. In 2009, he set an all-time record with his ninth consecutive season of 200 or more hits.

Unlike most players, Ichiro sports his first name on his jersey instead of his last.

SIMPLY THE BEST
Fans love to argue about which player is the best in terms of specific positions or skills. But nearly all of them—and most experts—agree that St. Louis Cardinals first baseman Albert Pujols is today's best overall player. Only once in his nine-year career has he finished lower than fourth in the MVP voting. He has season-home-run, RBI, and batting-average titles. He's an eight-time All-Star and one of the best clutch hitters in the game. Pujols was even a Gold Glove winner in 2006 for fielding excellence.

THE "DOC" IS IN
Starting pitchers are the workhorses of any Major League pitching staff. Their teams hope they can hold the opponent in check for many innings while the batters try to score runs behind him. Roy "Doc" Halladay of the Blue Jays is one of today's most effective. He's a six-time All-Star, a two-time 20-game winner, and a recipient of the 2003 Cy Young Award.

THREE CHEERS FOR THE FANS
More than 70 million people attended Major League Baseball games in 2009. In fact, nine teams topped 3 million fans each. That's on top of the millions who watch games at home on TV or online, or who listen on the radio. However, only the fans who sit the in the stands during games get a chance to try to catch a foul ball, as these Chicago Cubs fans are doing.

The Diamond

IF BASEBALL DIAMONDS WERE ANY OTHER SIZE, baseball might not work as well. But a baseball diamond is exactly 90 feet (27.4 m) on each side, which makes the game competitive for both teams. Each ground ball to the shortstop means a close play at first. Each double play is turned in the nick of time. And the time it takes a base stealer to go from first to second is just about the time it takes a pitcher to pitch and a catcher to throw down to second. Of course, a purist might note that a baseball diamond is actually a square viewed from one corner. But the shape is close enough that, at first, the area within the bases came to be called a diamond; soon, the entire field was known by this name. Beyond the base paths is the dirt, which, together with the central area, forms the infield. The outfield lies beyond this, made of grass or artificial turf. The outfield fences define the back of the field, while the foul lines extending from home plate define the sides. A diamond is much more than lines, fences, and bases, however. For many, a baseball diamond is the place where dreams come true.

DIAMONDS OF OLD
This photo of Griffith Stadium from 1933 shows that diamonds haven't changed much from earlier times. Like today, a wide dirt area separated the infield grass from the outfield grass. This view also shows the netting that ballparks put up behind home plate to protect fans from fast-moving foul balls or wild pitches.

Outfield fences can also be made of see-through mesh.

FAIR OR FOUL?
At the outfield end of the two foul lines are tall "foul poles." Any ball hit to the field side of the pole is fair; a ball hit to the outside of the pole is foul. Any ball that hits the foul pole is, ironically, fair. Most foul poles have nets (below) attached to the field side of the pole to help umpires make their calls.

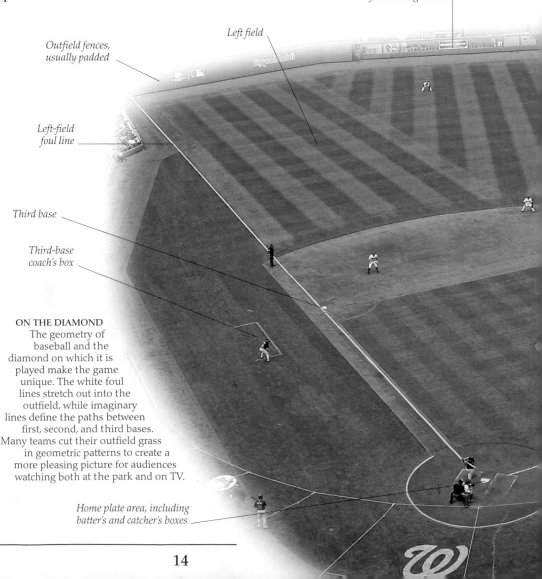

Left field

Outfield fences, usually padded

Left-field foul line

Third base

Third-base coach's box

ON THE DIAMOND
The geometry of baseball and the diamond on which it is played make the game unique. The white foul lines stretch out into the outfield, while imaginary lines define the paths between first, second, and third bases. Many teams cut their outfield grass in geometric patterns to create a more pleasing picture for audiences watching both at the park and on TV.

Home plate area, including batter's and catcher's boxes

A BALL CLUB'S SECOND HOME

The area where baseball teams sit during games when they're not on the field is called the dugout. Normally, dugouts are located at or below the level of the playing surface. Players wait on the bench for their turn to bat, or rest between innings in the field. In the dugout, players also get refreshments, discuss strategy with their coaches, and cheer on their teammates. In most stadiums, the dugouts lead directly to the locker rooms, where teams dress before the game and shower afterward.

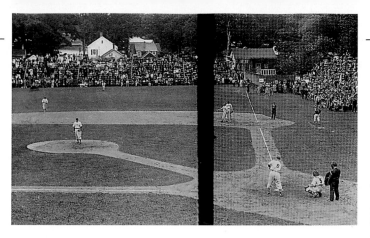

PATH TO THE PLATE

This photo from the 1930s shows two things now only rarely seen at ballparks: a dirt path between the pitcher's mound and home plate (today, Arizona's Chase Field and Detroit's Comerica Park have this old-time look) and obstructed-view seats. Fans unfortunate enough to sit behind the steel-beam upright (center) would have a hard time seeing some plays. Modern stadiums are constructed without such obstructions.

AT THE CENTER

Near the center of every diamond's infield is the pitcher's mound. Rules call for it to be 18 feet (5.5 m) in diameter and 10 inches (25 cm) above the level of home plate. The 24-by-6- inch (61 by 15 cm) pitching rubber is exactly 60 feet, 6 inches from home plate. A pitcher must be touching the rubber at the start of each pitch.

nter field

Second base

Some teams cut their logos in the outfield grass, as the Washington Nationals did here.

Right field

Warning track, made of dirt so outfielders can tell with their feet if they're approaching the wall.

Right-field foul line

First base

First-base coach's box

First base dugout

Coaches hit pregame warm-up grounders from these "fungo" circles.

Bats and balls

TAKE A STICK, THE LUMBER, a wand, or a toothpick. Combine it with a pearl, an apple, a pill, a rock, or a pea. What have you got? Everything you need to play baseball. Baseball bats and baseballs have earned many nicknames in the 150 years since the game started to become popular. And while many things have changed, the idea of hitting a round ball with a long, rounded stick has remained the same. The bats and balls used by Major League stars over the years have also become more than just the tools of their trade—they have become the stuff of legend, collected and treasured by generations of fans. Bats used by great players live in the Baseball Hall of Fame. Signed baseballs reside by the thousands on the shelves of fans around the world. And the ball that Mark McGwire hit for his 70th home run in 1998 sold to a private collector for $3 million. A pearl of great price, you might say.

WHAT THE PROS USE
Since 1977, the American and National Leagues have used this cow-leather covered ball made by Rawlings. Before then, the ball was sometimes covered with horsehide and made by Spalding. Home teams must supply five dozen new balls for each regular-season game. Umpires or clubhouse personnel "rub them up" with a special compound to erase factory shine.

FROM TREE TO BAT
The most famous model of wood bat used in the Majors is the Louisville Slugger, made by the Hillerich & Bradsby Company in Louisville, Kentucky. To make a bat, first a Northern white ash tree, at least 60 years old, is cut down. Trees less than 12 inches (30 cm) in diameter are cut into long pieces, or "splits." From the center of the split, the "square" is ripsawed. On a lathe, the square becomes a round cylinder. On another lathe, the bat is roughly shaped (note the extra pieces on the ends that hold the bat in place). In the next stage, the bat is sanded smooth. The finished product (below) is dipped in lacquer and then branded with the company's famous logo as well as the player's signature.

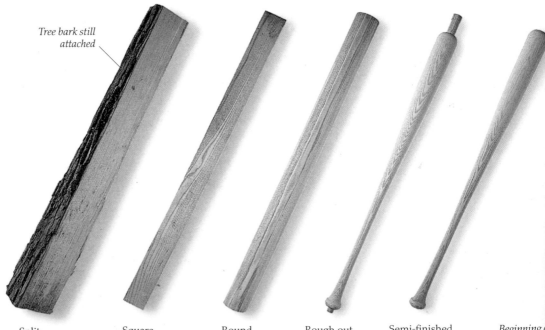

Tree bark still attached

Split Square Round Rough out Semi-finished *Beginning of barrel*

Knob *Handle*

INSIDE THE BASEBALL

Not every baseball is made like this one, but this is the baseball used at the highest level of play in the world: the Major Leagues. Official balls must weigh between 5 and 5¼ ounces (142–149 g). They must have a circumference of between 9 and 9¼ inches (22.8–23.5 cm). The lifespan of a Major League baseball during a game is about six pitches. Home-team personnel supply new balls as needed to the home plate umpire to put into play.

Cork and rubber

Black rubber

Red rubber

4-ply gray wool winding

3-ply white wool winding

4-ply gray wool winding

100 percent cotton finish winding

Full-grain, alum-tanned cowhide leather

Player's uniform number

5-ply waxed cotton thread, hand-stitched

THE BOTTLE BAT
The only player to successfully use this strange form of bat—thinner at the handle and uniformly wide along the barrel, instead of tapering as normal bats do—was Heinie Groh, who played for the Cincinnati Reds from 1913 to 1921.

Hollow barrel

IT GOES PING
The development of the aluminum bat in the early 1970s changed baseball at every level except the professional. Much sturdier than wood bats, aluminum bats last much longer and are almost impossible to break. Youth leagues, high schools, and colleges learned to love the cost efficiency of the aluminum bat. Purists bemoan its odd sound, and the effect aluminum has on batters. What would be simple outs with wood are singles with aluminum; what would be fly outs with wood turn into home runs. Still, more players today use aluminum than wood.

Signature of Ken Griffey, Jr. (H&B has thousands of cards on file with the bat preferences of Major Leaguers.)

AT THE BAT RACK
Baseball players take good care of their most important offensive tool: their bat. During the game, players store several bats in the bat rack in the dugout. A player might have half a dozen bats at the ready, in case one breaks during a game. Before the season, players get large shipments of bats made to their personal specifications; more can be ordered if necessary.

BALLPARK DONUTS
While warming up before hitting, some players slip this weighted ring, called a "donut," onto their bat. It fits over the knob but not the barrel. Swinging the bat with this added weight makes swinging seem easier and quicker when you take the weight off.

125 Louisville Slugger® Powerized
GENUINE C271
Ken Griffey Jr
SEATTLE MARINERS

Baseball gloves

Webbing

WHILE MANY THINGS ABOUT BASEBALL HAVE REMAINED nearly the same since the first games were played, one piece of equipment—the baseball glove—has undergone many changes. In fact, gloves were not even used regularly by players until the 1870s, as shown by the image at left. Even then, only the catcher wore one, and it was not much more than a leather glove with a bit of padding in the palm. Gloves (technically, only first basemen and catchers use "mitts") evolved slowly as more players began using them. The fingers were stitched together. The space between the thumb and forefinger was widened, creating a basket or pocket. The fingers got longer, the better to snare line drives. The leather got looser and more pliable, making the glove more comfortable, and gloves became more specialized for different positions. In the end, however, no matter how big or wide or high-tech a baseball glove is, it's only as useful as the hand inside it.

Pocket

Thumb

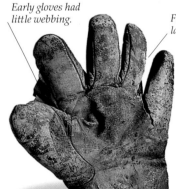

Early gloves had little webbing.

Fingers not laced together

IN THE OLD DAYS
Early gloves, such as this one from the 1920s, offered players little padding compared to today's gloves, and virtually no additional reach. Instead of snagging the ball in the web between the thumb and forefinger, as players usually do today, players back then had to grasp the ball to their palm with their fingers to catch it.

KIDS' GLOVES
Gloves for younger players are the same style as those used by pros, except they are smaller. Players young and old use their gloves to field grounders, as this infielder demonstrates. The glove's lacing and webbing create a wide "scoop" that makes this task easier.

JUST LIKE MICKEY
Major League players have long endorsed gloves, whether a replica of the model they use themselves or a kid-sized souvenir model like this one from the 1960s. Note the differences between the earlier model (above left) and this one, which has the fingers stitched together, and much wider webbing between the thumb and forefinger. Even so, the fingers are still not much bigger than on the hand.

*Laces holding
fingers together*

*Laces holding pieces
of glove together*

GOLD GLOVES
Since 1957, Major League players who excel with their gloves (and their throwing arms) are awarded the Gold Glove (left). There is one winner for each position in each league, including three prizes for outfielders.

CATCHER'S MITT
The most specialized baseball gloves are used by catchers. Features include extra padding in the pocket, extra-wide webbing, and an adjustable strap to ensure a tight fit. This particular glove is made with two colors of leather. Others are made with only one color, usually brown or black.

Model name

PITCHER'S GLOVE
The key to a pitcher's glove is secrecy. Pitchers use their gloves to hide the grip they are using on the ball until the last minute, so they don't give hitters any clue as to what they're throwing. While some outfielders' gloves have open webbing, pitchers always use gloves with closed webbing.

Finger sleeve

BIG BASKET AT FIRST
After the catcher's mitt, the first baseman's glove is the most unique. These gloves are longer and thinner than outfield gloves. They are more pointed at the top, the better to scoop low throws out of the dirt or to stretch out for throws that are off-line—here, Joey Votto of the Cincinnati Reds shows how this big basket makes catches easy. Also, first basemen learn to make catches that create an audible "pop" when the ball hits their mitt. Umpires often listen for the sound while watching the base for the runner's foot.

Heel

GLOVE STORY
his typical fielder's glove shows many of the features that make today's gloves o much better than baseball's first gloves. The large, secure webbing between he thumb and forefinger helps trap the ball; it's where most of the catches are nade. The longer fingers help players reach for balls hit or thrown to the side r over their heads. Padding in the heel and in the fingers helps cushion hard-hit balls. And specially chosen leather (left) makes each glove a soft and cushiony basket for making great catches.

Hats and helmets

THEY ARE CALLED BASEBALL CAPS, but golfers wear them on the golf course, race-car drivers wear them after races, and football quarterbacks and coaches wear them on the sidelines. And these days, it seems as if everyone in the nonsports world wears them, too. Baseball caps are the game's most important contribution to fashion. While baseball players wear caps for team identity and to keep the sun out of their eyes, many other sports have adopted the distinctive crown and bill of a baseball cap for use in their own games. Major League players wear very durable, high-quality hats fitted to each player's head. (When you're in the big leagues, you don't have to deal with those plastic clips at the back of your cap.) As for baseball helmets, they are a much more recent addition to the game. While a few players tried some form of helmet in the game's early years, it was only after the development of hard plastic during World War II that a durable and comfortable helmet could be made. Today, baseball players at all levels must wear helmets to protect their heads while batting.

Hard plastic, usually in team color

Ear hole

EXTRA PROTECTION
Many youth leagues now insist that batters wear face guards such as this one, along with plastic batting helmets with ear flaps on both sides. Face guards are designed to protect a batter's face from both pitches and foul tips, while also allowing good visibility. Although they can be awkward and uncomfortable, they can also be very helpful, especially to inexperienced players looking for confidence at the plate.

CHANGING TIMES
Just as styles in fashion change through time, so too do caps change in baseball. While a few teams have left their cap styles unchanged, these Baltimore Orioles' caps show how teams change colors, logos, and design through the years. In addition, this is a great way to sell more souvenir caps, as fans try to keep up with their heroes.

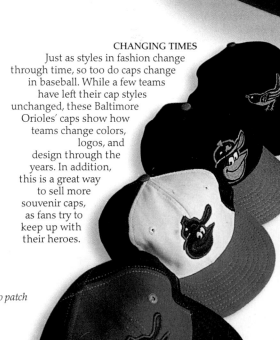

Team-logo patch

EARLY MAJOR LEAGUE HELMETS
The first helmets used in the Major Leagues were little more than hard plastic versions of the baseball cap, as modeled here by Minnesota Twins slugger Harmon Killebrew (573 career home runs). These helmets had little padding and afforded little protection.

Orioles' logo

SAFETY ON TOP
Although plastic batting helmets have been around since the 1950s, it was only in 1971 that they became mandatory in the Major Leagues. Pro players can wear models with only one ear flap (facing the pitcher), while players at other levels wear helmets with two ear flaps. The reason for batting helmets is simple: Being hit in the head with a pitch can be very dangerous. Many players' careers have been shortened after such "beanballs," as they are called. Only one Major League player has died as a result of "beanballs"—Ray Chapman in 1920. The heads of today's players are well-protected.

Strap attached rubber device to cap.

Brim

AN UNPOPULAR FIRST TRY
Players in early baseball didn't have the advantage of plastic. One enterprising company tried marketing this air-filled rubber bladder as a helmet. It attached to the player's cap with an elastic strap. Unfortunately, it was ineffective and didn't catch on.

A MOST TRADITIONAL TOPPER
Baseball caps, such as this one from the Santa Barbara Foresters national-championship summer team, are as much about tradition as function. Caps keep the sun out of a player's eyes, but then what is their purpose at night? Or in an indoor stadium? Since the game began, wearing the cap is as much a part of being a ballplayer as swinging a bat. Caps normally are made of six triangular panels held together by a fabric-covered, galvanized-steel button at the top. The team logo is on the front of the cap.

Foam padding

Snap for chin strap, sometimes used in youth baseball.

Ventilation holes

ROM THE OLD DAYS
his New York Giants' ap from 1922 shows ow baseball caps have hanged only slightly ver the years. The rimary changes have ome in the height of e crown and the ngth of the bill. Early ps were worn more ugly on the top of the ead, while bills were a t shorter.

Brim, usually fabric stitched over heavy cardboard.

Uniforms

THE MAIN REASON FOR UNIFORMS IS SIMPLE—to show who is on what team. Baseball uniforms are designed to allow freedom of movement and comfort as the player plays the game. Mimicking the first uniforms, modern outfits consist of a short-sleeved shirt (often worn over a longer-sleeved undershirt), pants with a belt, and a baseball cap. Today, however, baseball uniforms are made of tight-fitting, stretchy polyester and other synthetic fabrics. Early uniforms were made of heavy wool that got heavier as the game went on and the players sweated. The pants were originally designed to stop just below the knee. But today's Major Leaguers almost always prefer much longer pants, even while bucking tradition. Unfortunately, these long pants hide another unique part of the baseball uniform: stirrup socks worn over white socks. As with all sports equipment, the uniform is not as important as what the player does while he's wearing it.

Fitted cap

Year made (1952), size (4 and player's number (9)

SUPERSTAR SHIRT AND SHOES
Each team has a unique design on its jerseys. This home Red Sox jersey belonged to the great Ted Williams. Boston has not changed its basic logo for decades, but other teams have changed their looks and logos several times. Williams's baseball shoes (below) show that the basic configuration of the metal spikes (three-pronged triangles at front and back) has not changed much since the "Splendid Splinter" wore these in the 1950s.

Leather uppers

Metal spikes tacked to soles

Early caps had very low crowns…

…and very short bills.

Longer sleeves

Leather belt

Pants fall to just below knees.

High socks, before stirrups

STAR MODELS
Detroit's Hall of Fame outfielder Ty Cobb (left) and "Shoeless" Joe Jackson of the Cleveland Naps model uniforms worn in the Majors before World War I. Compare the baggy wool pants and jerseys to the sleek, tight-fitting uniforms of today's players. The thick wool of the uniforms made keeping them clean difficult, and they were almost permanently stained with grass and dirt.

WEARIN' O' THE GREEN
Spring training is a time for fun. Each March 17, as clubs play exhibition games in Florida and Arizona, several teams celebrate St. Patrick's Day by donning special green-trimmed uniforms. This one, complete with a shamrock on the sleeve, was worn by Hall of Fame pitcher Tom Seaver when he was with the Cincinnati Reds. For one day each spring, the team becomes the Cincinnati Greens.

Batting helmet
with ear flap

White home
jersey

Elbow pad

Batting glove

CLASSIC PINSTRIPES

All-Star shortstop Derek Jeter of the New York Yankees models one of baseball's classic uniforms: the Yankee pinstripes. These uniforms, worn at home by the Bronx Bombers, have barely changed in color and logo from the days of Mickey Mantle and Yogi Berra, but have greatly changed in style. Like all modern baseball uniforms, they are body-hugging, stretch polyester made for comfort, durability, and protection. Teams have a different uniform for road games, usually in a basic gray and featuring their city name instead of their team name. As in the old days, a baseball uniform consists of a jersey, pants, hat, and socks. Most players today, however, wear long pants instead of knee-length knickers.

Jeter, like many players, wears baseball cleats that cover the ankles for more support.

RETIRED NUMBERS

Teams "retire" jersey numbers to honor their greatest heroes. No Giants player, for instance, will ever wear Willie Mays's number 24 again.

OLD IS NEW AGAIN

Several times each season, teams wear special uniforms. Some are "throwbacks," celebrating what teams looked like long ago. Other teams honor Negro League teams from the past, such as these Detroit Tigers-turned-Detroit Stars from 2009.

BENEATH THE UNI

Padded "sliding shorts" are often worn over the player's athletic supporter or underwear. The fabric is stretchy with lightly padded outer thighs.

Pitching

Four-seam fastball

Two-seam fastball

Curveball

"Circle" change-up

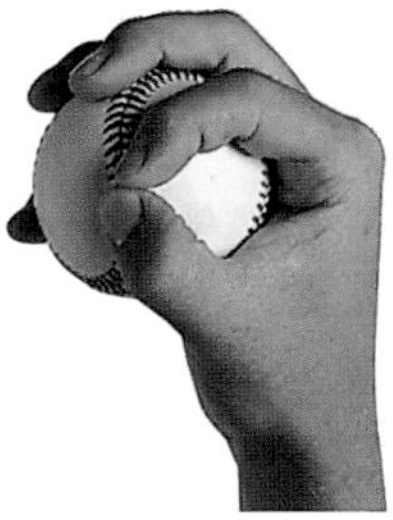

Knuckleball

THE PITCHER'S MOUND is the center of the baseball universe. Nothing happens in a baseball game until the pitcher starts his windup and fires in that first pitch. His job is to get the opposing hitters out, but saying that and doing it are two very different things. Warren Spahn (363 wins, the most by a left-hander) said, "Hitting is the art of timing. Pitching is the art of upsetting timing." A wide variety of pitch types (left) are used to upset a hitter's timing. An even wider variety of arm motions, leg motions, and body spins have also been put to use over the years. And until the 1920s, pitchers could legally deface a ball by cutting it or applying all sorts of "foreign substances" (including spit) to make it harder to hit. It's a tough job—pitchers need all the help they can get.

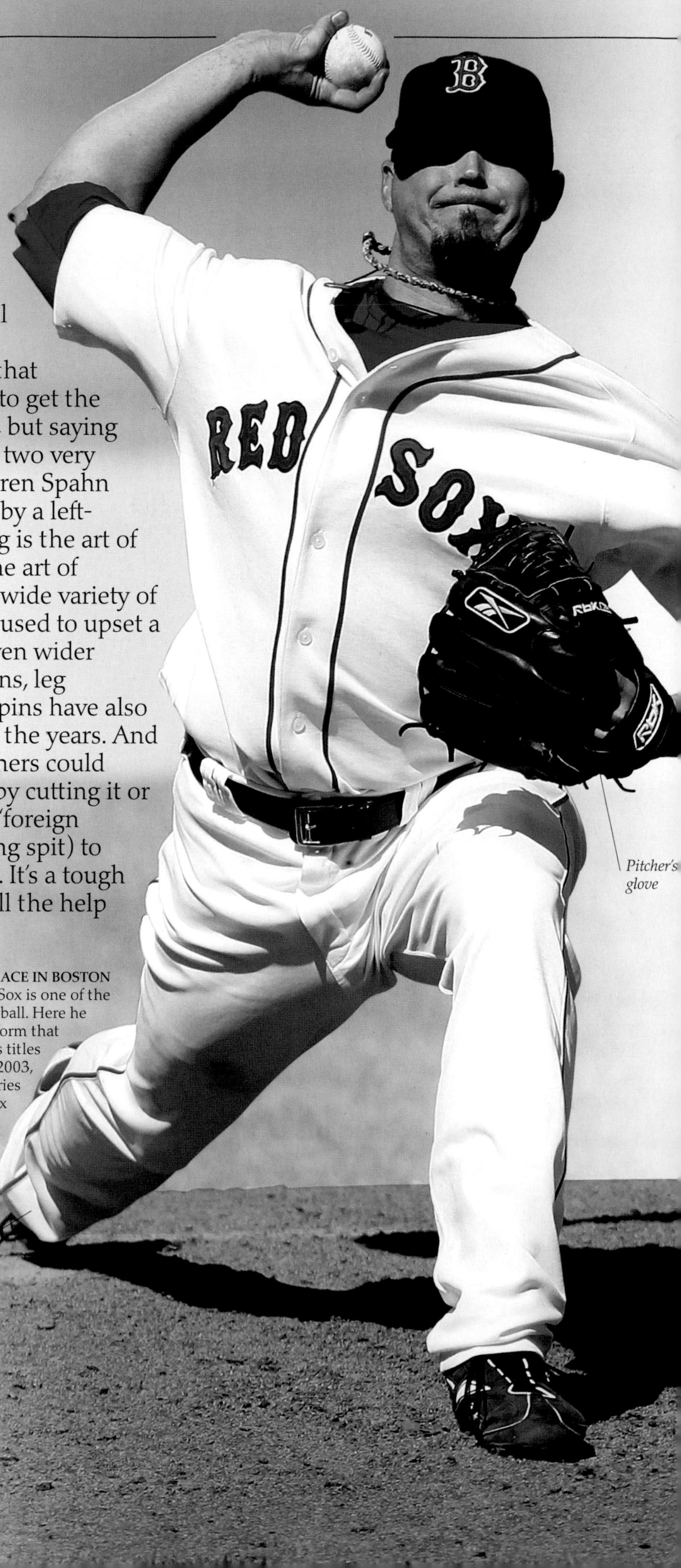

AN ACE IN BOSTON
Josh Beckett of the Boston Red Sox is one of the best starting pitchers in baseball. Here he shows off the near-perfect form that helped him win World Series titles with the Florida Marlins (2003, when he was also World Series MVP) and with the Red Sox (2007). Teams rely on "aces" like Beckett to anchor their pitching rotations.

Pitcher's glove

Pitchers drive toward home by pushing off the pitching rubber with their back foot.

GETTING A GRIP
Different pitches are thrown using different grips (above). Pitchers determine how a ball moves or curves by changing the position of their fingers on the raised seams of the ball, or by turning their wrist.

Hand behind head

Arm whips forward

Follow-through

Ready to field

Start position

The stride

Driving off back foot

GOING THROUGH THE MOTION

If hitting, as many players claim, is one of the "hardest things in sports," then pitching is a close second. Pitchers all have their own styles of "delivery," but whether they throw over the top, from three-quarters, or sidearm, they all have one aim—throw the ball past the hitter in the strike zone. All pitchers have two basic deliveries: the set delivery, used when there are men on base, and the windup, used when the bases are empty. The first of these helps deliver the ball more quickly, reducing the time in which runners can attempt steals.

FROM A NO-NO

This ball was used in 1938 by Reds pitcher Johnny Vander Meer in the first of his record two consecutive no-hitters. Those are the rare games in which the pitchers on one team do not allow a hit.

511

Watching many of baseball's legendary records fall (Hank Aaron's 755 homers, Lou Gehrig's 2,130 consecutive games played, Ty Cobb's 4,189 hits), it would be easy to say that any record is breakable. One that most assuredly is not is the career victory total of Denton True "Cy" Young, who earned 511 wins from 1890 to 1911. He won more than 30 games in a season five times. He combined durability with power and guile to dominate baseball's early years. Today, the annual A.L. and N.L. awards for best pitcher are named after him.

Flimsy non-webbed glove

FIVE FABULOUS SEASONS

From 1962 to 1966, Sandy Koufax of the Dodgers was the greatest pitcher of all time. The left-hander's sizzling fastball and devastating curve yielded three Cy Young Awards, five ERA titles, and four no-hitters. His 27 wins in 1966 were the most by an N.L. lefty in the 20th century. Sadly, arthritis forced him to retire after that season.

Baggy wool uniform

Fastball grip

High-topped shoes

UNUSUAL DELIVERY

A pitcher's throwing motion is called his "delivery." San Francisco's Tim Lincecum has one of the most unusual in the game—but one of the most effective, too. He was the 2008 N.L. Cy Young Award winner and is a two-time strikeout champ.

IT'S ALL ABOUT SPEED

More so than ever before, pitchers are judged by how fast they can throw the ball. Movement and control are vital, too, but speed rules. Few baseball scouts go anywhere without a radar gun (left) to measure pitch speed. You probably won't reach the Major Leagues unless your fastball reaches 90 miles per hour (145 km/h). Hit 100 and you earn a fast-track ticket to "the Show" (the big leagues).

Catching

PLAY AT THE PLATE!
One of baseball's most exciting plays occurs when ball and runner arrive at home plate at the same time. The catcher must block the plate and make the tag. Here, Jorge Posada of the Yankees does just that, keeping the Orioles' Melvin Mora from reaching home.

T HE HARDEST-WORKING PLAYER on a baseball team is the catcher. Squatting behind home plate for nine innings, he must catch everything a pitcher throws past a hitter, endure being hit by foul tips and bats, and be ready to fire perfect throws to cut down would-be base stealers. Occasionally, he must deal with charging runners who plow into him like a football fullback, or soothe a pitcher's shattered ego after a home run. The great Yankees manager Casey Stengel summed up the importance of the catcher when he said, "You've gotta have a catcher. If you don't have a catcher, you're going to have a lot of passed balls."

Yogi Berra

JUST LIKE THE PROS
Playing catcher in a youth baseball league is just as grueling as playing in the pros. Like their Major League role models, young catchers wear all the protective gear available, including masks, helmets, chest protectors, shin guards, and protective cups. It sometimes takes young players a while to adjust to the gear, but after a few foul tips, they'll find it's worth the effort.

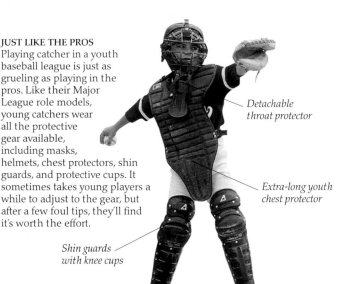

Detachable throat protector

Extra-long youth chest protector

Shin guards with knee cups

CAMPY
After six seasons in the Negro Leagues, Roy Campanella joined the Brooklyn Dodgers in 1948 and redefined the catching position. Combining power at the plate with great catching skills, "Campy" won three MVP awards in the 1950s. Sadly, a 1958 car accident left him partially paralyzed. However, he remained close to the game and was one of baseball's most beloved figures until his death in 1993.

Campanella in 1950s Wheaties ad

EARLY CAGES
Most catcher's equipment has changed only in materials rather than form. The mask is a good example. This 1930s mask has a padded frame and criss-crossing metal bars to keep the ball from hitting the catcher's face. Today's masks (main photo) are similar, with improved padding and stronger bars, plus the addition of helmets to protect the back of the head.

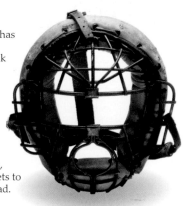

CATCHING WITH A PILLOW
Early catcher's mitts (right) were little more than round leather pillows with space for the hand to fit into the back. The pocket was developed over time by catching the ball. There was little or no hinge or webbing. Most catchers needed to use both hands to catch. Modern gloves (opposite, top right) have made catching safer by letting catchers use only one hand.

Very small webbing area

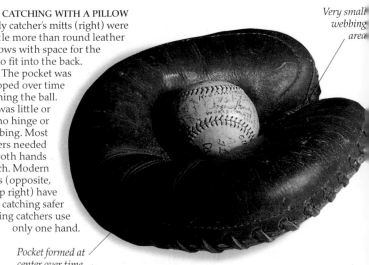

Pocket formed at center over time

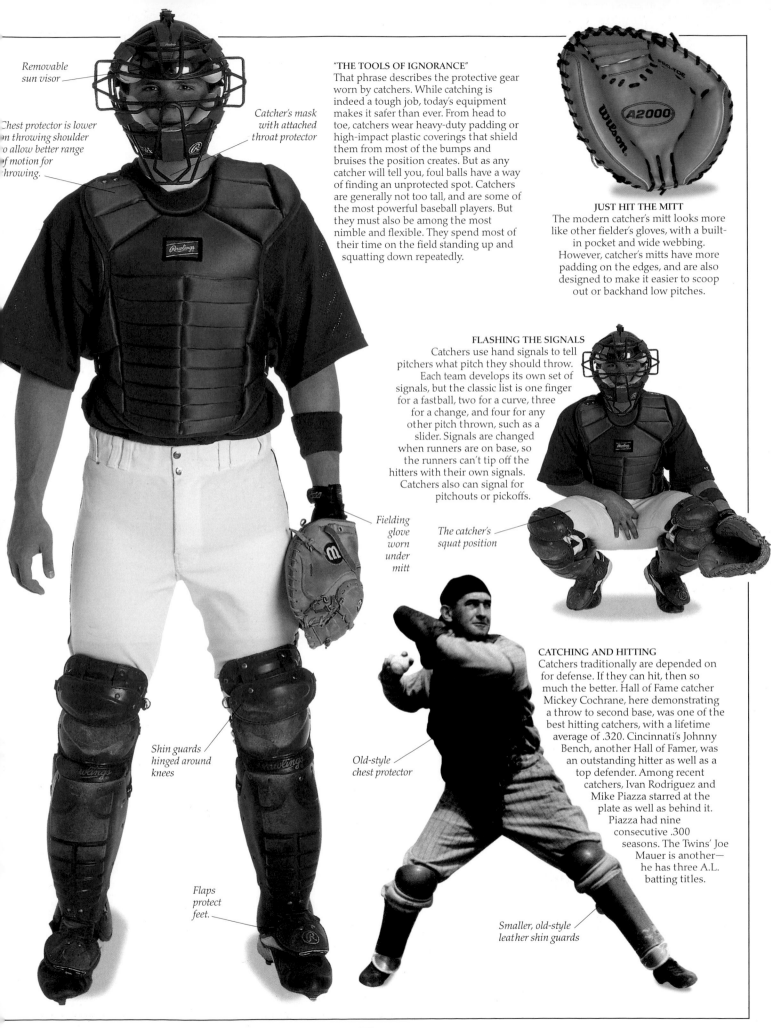

Removable
sun visor

Chest protector is lower
on throwing shoulder
to allow better range
of motion for
throwing.

Catcher's mask
with attached
throat protector

Fielding
glove
worn
under
mitt

Shin guards
hinged around
knees

Flaps
protect
feet.

Old-style
chest protector

Smaller, old-style
leather shin guards

"THE TOOLS OF IGNORANCE"

That phrase describes the protective gear worn by catchers. While catching is indeed a tough job, today's equipment makes it safer than ever. From head to toe, catchers wear heavy-duty padding or high-impact plastic coverings that shield them from most of the bumps and bruises the position creates. But as any catcher will tell you, foul balls have a way of finding an unprotected spot. Catchers are generally not too tall, and are some of the most powerful baseball players. But they must also be among the most nimble and flexible. They spend most of their time on the field standing up and squatting down repeatedly.

JUST HIT THE MIT

The modern catcher's mitt looks more like other fielder's gloves, with a built-in pocket and wide webbing. However, catcher's mitts have more padding on the edges, and are also designed to make it easier to scoop out or backhand low pitches.

FLASHING THE SIGNALS

Catchers use hand signals to tell pitchers what pitch they should throw. Each team develops its own set of signals, but the classic list is one finger for a fastball, two for a curve, three for a change, and four for any other pitch thrown, such as a slider. Signals are changed when runners are on base, so the runners can't tip off the hitters with their own signals. Catchers also can signal for pitchouts or pickoffs.

The catcher's
squat position

CATCHING AND HITTING

Catchers traditionally are depended on for defense. If they can hit, then so much the better. Hall of Fame catcher Mickey Cochrane, here demonstrating a throw to second base, was one of the best hitting catchers, with a lifetime average of .320. Cincinnati's Johnny Bench, another Hall of Famer, was an outstanding hitter as well as a top defender. Among recent catchers, Ivan Rodriguez and Mike Piazza starred at the plate as well as behind it. Piazza had nine consecutive .300 seasons. The Twins' Joe Mauer is another— he has three A.L. batting titles.

Infield and outfield

On DEFENSE, A BASEBALL TEAM has two parts: infield and outfield. The four players who play near the bases form the infield. The three players who play out beyond the bases are the outfield. (The pitcher and catcher are also officially part of the infield.) Each of the infield positions—first base, second base, shortstop, and third base—has an area of responsibility as well as skills particular to that area. The three outfield spots—left field, center field, and right field—are more similar. No matter what their specialty, all of these players have one job when the ball is put into play: Get the runners out to stop runs from being scored.

OUTFIELD THROWS
Outfielders use a special throwing motion to get the ball in to the proper base or cutoff man. Atlanta outfielder Jordan Schafer shows how an outfielder uses a very long stride and a strong overhand arm motion to create a hard, low, line-drive throw. They also try to use the momentum they gain by charging in to catch the ball to add power to their throws. Right fielders normally have the strongest throwing arm in the outfield because they have to make the longest throws, from deep in right field to third base.

SHOESTRING CATCH
Outfielders must catch anything hit in the air, even if it means running dozens of yards to nab the ball just before it hits the ground. Players such as Mike Cameron of the Milwaukee Brewers (above) learn to judge where a ball will land almost from the instant it leaves the bat. Speed and timing are vital for outfielders.

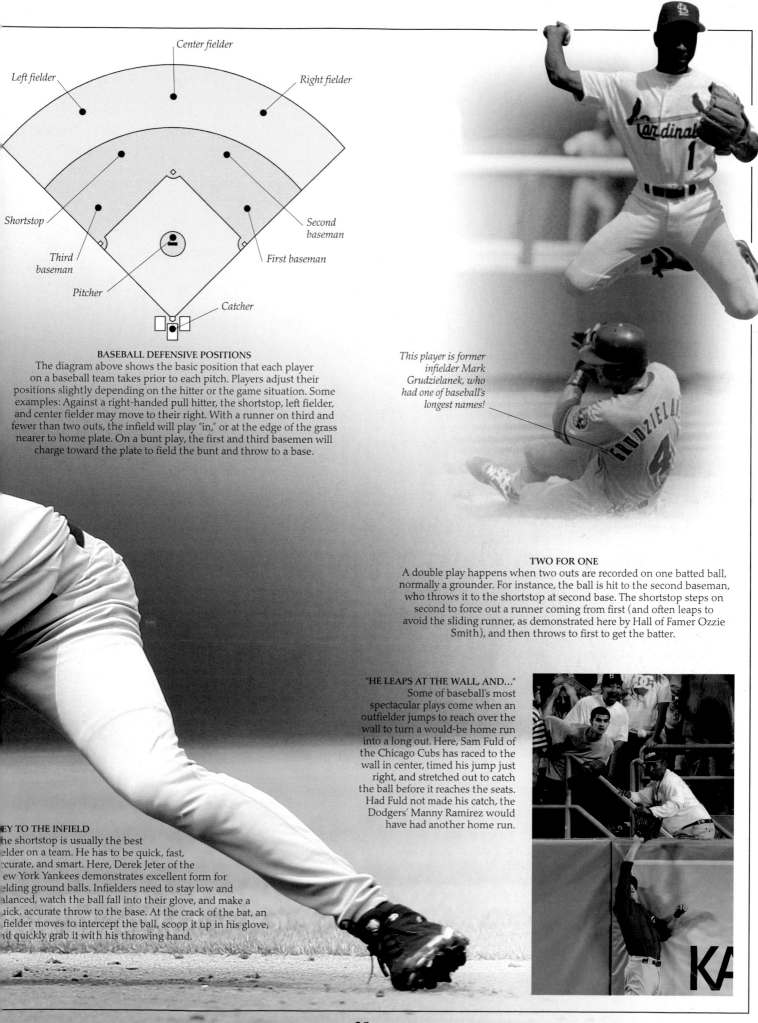

Center fielder

Left fielder

Right fielder

Shortstop

Second baseman

Third baseman

First baseman

Pitcher

Catcher

BASEBALL DEFENSIVE POSITIONS

The diagram above shows the basic position that each player on a baseball team takes prior to each pitch. Players adjust their positions slightly depending on the hitter or the game situation. Some examples: Against a right-handed pull hitter, the shortstop, left fielder, and center fielder may move to their right. With a runner on third and fewer than two outs, the infield will play "in," or at the edge of the grass nearer to home plate. On a bunt play, the first and third basemen will charge toward the plate to field the bunt and throw to a base.

This player is former infielder Mark Grudzielanek, who had one of baseball's longest names!

TWO FOR ONE

A double play happens when two outs are recorded on one batted ball, normally a grounder. For instance, the ball is hit to the second baseman, who throws it to the shortstop at second base. The shortstop steps on second to force out a runner coming from first (and often leaps to avoid the sliding runner, as demonstrated here by Hall of Famer Ozzie Smith), and then throws to first to get the batter.

"HE LEAPS AT THE WALL, AND..."

Some of baseball's most spectacular plays come when an outfielder jumps to reach over the wall to turn a would-be home run into a long out. Here, Sam Fuld of the Chicago Cubs has raced to the wall in center, timed his jump just right, and stretched out to catch the ball before it reaches the seats. Had Fuld not made his catch, the Dodgers' Manny Ramirez would have had another home run.

EY TO THE INFIELD

he shortstop is usually the best elder on a team. He has to be quick, fast, ccurate, and smart. Here, Derek Jeter of the ew York Yankees demonstrates excellent form for elding ground balls. Infielders need to stay low and alanced, watch the ball fall into their glove, and make a uick, accurate throw to the base. At the crack of the bat, an fielder moves to intercept the ball, scoop it up in his glove, d quickly grab it with his throwing hand.

Batting

Stan Musial used his odd batting style to total 3,630 hits, fourth all-time.

Ask anyone who has tried it: Hitting a baseball is the single most difficult feat in sports. The greatest hitters—or batters, the terms are interchangeable—succeed only about three times out of ten. A basketball player with that success rate would be out of a job; a field-goal kicker wouldn't make the football team; a hockey goalie would be job-shopping. But batting is so hard to do well that .300 is the gold standard. In less than a third of a second, batters must decide to swing, begin their swing, and then, another tiny fraction of a second later, somehow connect a rounded bat with a wildly spinning ball that is flying toward them at speeds that can reach more than 90 miles per hour. It's hard to do, but when it's done well, wow . . . what a singularly thrilling moment.

Ready to hit

Shoulder turn begins

Eyes on the ball

Wrists turn over

Full follow-through

IT SURE *LOOKS* EASY
This sequence of photos shows proper, classic hitting form. However, each player adapts this basic form to his or her needs and particular abilities. Some players will begin the swing with the bat higher or lower, or will take a short or long step with their front foot. The keys to a successful swing, though, are the same no matter what style a batter uses: consistency, keeping the eyes on the ball, and remaining smooth and quick throughout. Put all these things together, swing at the right pitch, and a hit is often the result.

Cobb played in the days before batting helmets.

THE GEORGIA PEACH
Hall of Fame outfielder Ty Cobb held his hands several inches apart on the bat, a style that no one has successfully imitated. No one could match his talent, either. Cobb used that odd style to compile a Major League record .366 lifetime average and 4,189 hits, second-most all-time.

OH, WHAT A HITTER
The Major Leagues are not the only place to find great hitters. Sadaharu Oh of the Tokyo Giants used his unusual batting style— lifting his right leg as he strode into the pitch—to hit an international record 868 career home runs in nearly 600 fewer at-bats than Major League career leader Barry Bonds.

YOOK!
Boston's Kevin Youkilis has one of the oddest swings in the game today. He starts with his right hand way up the bat. It doesn't join the left hand until he brings the bat to the point shown here. He also lifts his leg to create a bigger drive.

Bat cocked toward pitcher

High kick with front leg

30

"THE GREATEST HITTER WHO EVER LIVED"
This sequence (clockwise from top left) shows the form of Ted Williams, the Red Sox outfielder whose childhood dream was to be the greatest hitter of all time. His dream came true. Williams posted a lifetime average of .344 with 521 home runs, even though he gave up five seasons to military service. Combining power, accuracy, and an unerring eye, the "Splendid Splinter" could flat-out hit.

This ball will probably be fouled back, since Martin just missed clean contact.

EYES ON THE BALL
This photo captures the exact moment that Dodgers catcher Russell Martin's bat meets the speeding baseball. Martin has his hands in front of his hips, and his weight has shifted to his front foot. His left arm is extended and his right arm will follow shortly He also has his head down, trying to watch the point of contact.

Youth-league face mask

Fingers cradle bat lightly to let bat "give" with the pitch.

Hips and shoulders square to face pitcher

Ventilated for comfort

FITS LIKE A GLOVE
While old-timers such as Cobb and Williams would have no use for them, batting gloves are essential for all but a handful of today's players. The leather-and-nylon gloves give players a surer grip on the bat.

LAY ONE DOWN, KID
A special type of hit is called the "bunt." In this move, the batter pushes the pitch softly so that it stays between the pitcher's mound and home plate. The batter usually is put out on a "sacrifice" bunt, but the runners on base advance.

Baserunning

ONCE A BATTER REACHES a base, he or she becomes a base runner. Being a good base runner is almost as important as being a good hitter. Base runners advance from base to base when their teammates put the ball in play. They also can advance by stealing a base or on a passed ball or wild pitch (when a pitch gets by the catcher). Every base runner has one goal: Step on home plate and score a run. A base runner must always be alert—how many outs are there? What's the count? Who is pitching? Where are the fielders? These variables change on every pitch. Concentration is as vital to a base runner as speed and technique.

KING OF THIEVES
One of the best base stealers in the game today is Tampa Bay's Carl Crawford. He has led the A.L. four times in steals, and has five season with 50 or more steals. His .295 career batting average helps him ge on base often, and his speed and daring mean he has the potential t steal at any time. He helped the Rays win the 2008 A.L. pennant.

GOTCHA!
Pitchers, catchers, and first basemen work together to make stealing bases harder. Both pitchers catchers can throw to bases, usually first, to keep base runners close. By reducing the runner's lead before the pitch this way, the defense makes it harder for the runner to steal. On this play, the Houston catcher fired the ball to first baseman Lance Berkman, who tagged the Pirates' Nyjer Morgan before he could return to first base.

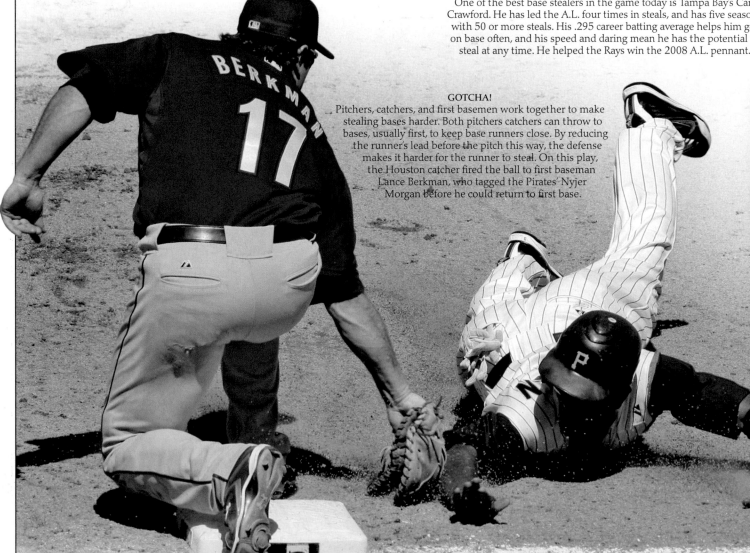

BARRIER BREAKER

Until Jackie Robinson joined the Brooklyn Dodgers in 1947, no African-American had played Major League Baseball since 1884. For decades, racism kept thousands of great athletes out of the game until the courageous Robinson and Dodgers' general manager Branch Rickey broke the barrier. Once he was in, Robinson quickly proved himself with his speed and daring on the base paths.

This card and the photo above both show Robinson stealing home.

Base runners keep their batting gloves on to protect their hands while sliding.

HEADFIRST

Most coaches and players say that sliding feet first (below) is easier and safer. However, some players use a headfirst dive into the base, demonstrated here by Emilio Bonifacio of the Florida Marlins.

Third-base coach

HE'S IN THERE!

One of the hardest things for young players to learn is the unique baseball skill of sliding. When running hard toward a base, sliding on the dirt is the only way for a runner to safely reduce his momentum and keep from going past the base. A good slide—as demonstrated here by Derrek Lee of the Cubs, sliding into third—involves keeping one leg extended toward the base, with the other tucked underneath. Some players drag the hand farthest from the base for balance.

HOME RUN TROT

A base runner's favorite turn around the bases is after a home run. Then the runner, in this case Detroit's Curtis Granderson, gets to take his time jogging from base to base. They get to high-five their base coaches as they make the trip. Batters can also circle the bases on an inside-the-park home run, in which the ball never leaves the playing field but is hit far enough to let a speedy slugger score.

Base runners are required to keep their helmets on to protect them from errant throws.

Cubs players wear patches featuring bear cubs.

Managers and coaches

IN A FAMOUS BASEBALL MOVIE, a team manager says, "This is a simple game: You throw the ball, you hit the ball, you catch the ball." Kids can figure that part out. However, managers and coaches are still needed to organize, lead, teach, and guide baseball teams from Little League on up to the pros. Pro teams have a manager who is in charge of everything that happens on the field. He makes the lineup, chooses pitchers, and calls plays. He is usually assisted by a pitching coach, a hitting coach, and base coaches, and sometimes by other specialists or assistants. Most coaches are former players who pass their knowledge on to younger ones. But managers and coaches also have to help young men grow up as well as throw, hit, and catch.

NAP'S CAP
Hall of Fame infielder Napoleon Lajoie wore this cap while managing the Cleveland team in the A.L. He was so popular that, while he led the team, they were called the Naps.

FLASHING THE SIGNS
When a team is at bat, a coach (right) stands beside first and third bases. He relays orders about hitting and baserunning from the manager to batters and base runners. Most coaches use a secret serie of signals, touches, claps, and movements. This prevents the opponent from knowing what a team is planning.

BACKING UP HIS PLAYERS
When a manager or coach argues with an umpire, he is certainly disputing the call. But he is also playing an important leadership role, defending the actions of his players and doing everything he can to help them win. By arguing himself, he can also prevent his players from getting in trouble.

EYES ON THE GAME

Along with the manager, teams employ veteran coaches. Here, pitching coach Mark Wiley and hitting coach Jim Presley watch the game from the Marlins dugout. These experts work with the players in their areas of expertise, and also advise the manager on key decisions.

SETTING THE LINEUP

The manager's most obvious job is filling out the lineup for his team. Before the game, he presents a lineup card like the one at right to the umpires and the opposing manager (below). The card shows the team's batting order and also keeps track of reserves who might enter the game later. A manager uses many lineups during a season to give his teams the best chances of winning each game.

Home-plate umpire

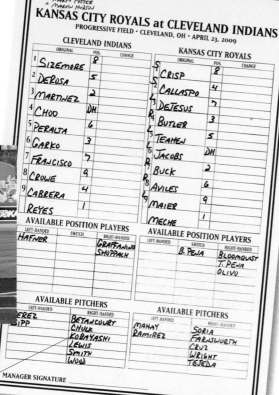

Reserve players are listed on the bottom of the lineup card.

FROM PLAYER TO LEADER

Of the 34 managers in the Major Leagues in 2009, more than half started out as Major League players. These managers can sometimes get more respect from their team, since they've gone through what the players are going through. Ozzie Guillen (right) of the Chicago White Sox is one of these players-turned-managers. His fiery style of leadership comes from his experience as a player. He leads in the way that he wanted to be led when he played the game.

SORRY, KID, GOTTA TAKE YOU OUT

The manager's most visible role in most games is to visit the pitching mound and take a struggling pitcher out of a game. Here, the Yankees' infielders and catcher Jorge Posada have gathered around pitcher Mike Dunn as manager Joe Girardi (27) approaches to take the ball. How a manager organizes his pitching staff during and between games is one of his most important responsibilities. Choosing the right pitcher to face a certain opponent, or deciding when to make a change can mean the difference between victory and defeat—or between keeping his job and looking for a new one.

Hey, Blue!

BASEBALL IS A GAME OF RULES, and the people charged with enforcing those rules are called umpires. Umpires determine, or "call," whether a pitch is a ball or a strike, they call base runners safe or out, and they decide whether a batted ball is foul or fair. In the Major Leagues, four umpires are used in regular-season games, and six are used in the playoffs and World Series. One of the four "umps" works behind home plate, while the others are stationed at each of the three bases. At lower levels of baseball, anywhere from one to four umpires are used. Umpires have a tough job. Baseball is a fast-moving game, so umps must make split-second decisions that can mean victory or defeat for one team or the other. Why "Hey, Blue"? Although some Major League umpires now wear black, their uniforms were originally navy blue. So no matter what his actual name is, any baseball umpire will respond to the name "Blue."

OLD-TIME GEAR
Until the 1970s, American League home-plate umpires wore large chest protectors outside their coats. This model from the 1930s was bulky, made of heavy leather, and hard to manage. Today's umpires wear thinner, lighter gear under their uniform shirts.

THE BRUSH OFF
Umpires need a clean, clear view of home plate. The home-plate umpire carries a small brush (an older model is pictured) to wipe off the plate periodically. Umpires always turn their back to the field before bending down and dusting.

Thumb wheel

KEEPING TRACK
All umpires carry handheld "indicators" (older model, left; newer version, right) that help them keep track of the number of outs, balls, strikes, and innings. While fans look to scoreboards for this information, the umpires have the final say.

THE RHUBARB
Every judgment call by an umpire upsets at least one of the two teams in the game. When a team's manager is especially upset, he comes on to the field to argue with the umpire. The ensuing "rhubarb" can be a tense discussion, like this one with Dusty Baker, manager of the Reds, or a hat-flinging, dust-kicking screaming match. Managers and players are supposed to be ejected for arguing about balls and strikes.

Indication of ejection

Dark blue shirt

Gray pants

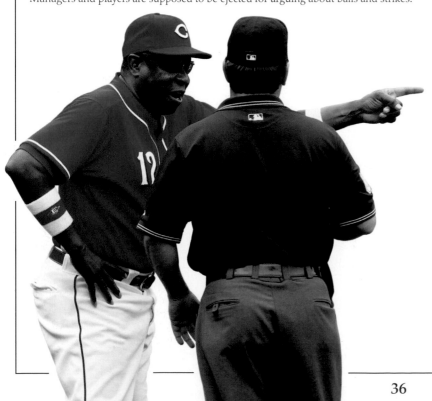

YOU'RE OUTTA HERE!
When an umpire feels a player or manager has argued too much or has stepped beyond the bounds of sportsmanship, he ejects that manager or player from the game. The ejected person must leave the dugout and return to the clubhouse. The leagues may also impose fines or additional suspensions for particularly bad sportsmanship.

Sun visor

Face mask

Shoulder pads
protect ump from
foul tips.

Chest
protector is
under shirt.

Ball
bag

Steel-toed
shoes

BEHIND THE PLATE

The home-plate umpire has the toughest job on the umpiring crew.
He must make split second decisions on whether a pitch is a ball or strike,
judge any bunts fair or foul, and make calls on close plays at the plate. Each
home-plate umpire develops his own personal style for calling strikes. Some
are subtle; some are loud and dramatic. The home-plate umpire wears
protective gear, including a chest protector, face mask,
shin guards, and heavy shoes.

HE'S OUT!

Just as home-plate umpires develop personal
strike calls, base umpires develop their own
unique ways of calling a player "out." This
umpire demonstrates the classic "punch-out"
style after the fielder has applied the tag to the
runner. Other umps use an outstretched
thumb on one hand.

HE'S IN THERE!

This umpire shows he has called the runner "safe" by spreading his arms wide.
According to legend, hand signals were first developed to help a deaf player
named "Dummy" Hoy, who couldn't hear the umpires' vocal calls. However,
modern historians have shown that this story is false.

FAIR OR FOUL?

Umpires at first and third base determine if batted balls are fair or foul.
This umpire is indicating a fair ball by pointing toward fair territory. The ball
must hit the ground within the white line to be fair.

Cards and stats

Baseball without statistics would be like chocolate milk without chocolate. The thousands of numbers that swirl around baseball like confetti are the lifeblood of the game. Stats allow fans to compare players of today and yesterday; to marvel at 500 home runs or 300 wins; to argue whether Randy Johnson could out-pitch Walter Johnson; to support a claim that Jackie Robinson was better than Joe Morgan. Baseball has stats for everything from pitching to hitting to baserunning. You might not ever need to know how well a player hits left-handers in night road games in June with less than two outs, but in baseball, you can find that out if you really want to. One of the ways that fans keep track of all these stats is with baseball cards. These little rectangles of cardboard have helped fans follow the careers of their heroes since the pro game began in the 1870s. While every sport has cards now, baseball had them first.

EARLY CARDBOARD HEROES
The card on the left features ace pitcher Mordecai "Three-Finger" Brown (1903–16). Although a childhood accident cost him parts of two fingers, he finished his career with a 2.06 career ERA, third-lowest all-time. On the right is Michael "King" Kelly, who was, until Babe Ruth came along, the most famous baseball player in America. He played for four teams from 1878 to 1893, earned the highest salary of the day, and had a famous song composed in his honor—"Slide, Kelly, Slide."

NO SMOKING
This piece of cardboard is worth more than $2.8 million. Only a handful of copies of this 1910 Honus Wagner card exist, and its rarity, along with the popularity of card collecting, have helped drive its value up. Originally sold with packs of tobacco, this card is rare because Wagner asked that his image not be used to promote tobacco. The few cards that did make it onto the market have become the most valuable in the sports-card world.

Although he is remembered as a second baseman, Robinson played outfield in 1954.

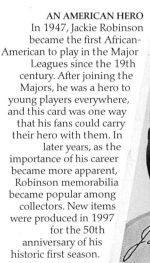

AN AMERICAN HERO
In 1947, Jackie Robinson became the first African-American to play in the Major Leagues since the 19th century. After joining the Majors, he was a hero to young players everywhere, and this card was one way that his fans could carry their hero with them. In later years, as the importance of his career became more apparent, Robinson memorabilia became popular among collectors. New items were produced in 1997 for the 50th anniversary of his historic first season.

Signature printed on card

A CLASSIC COMPANY
Over the years, many companies have produced baseball cards. They sign contracts with Major League Baseball or the MLB Players' Association and the players share in the money the cards earn. The Topps Company is the oldest and best-known one currently operating. Topps produced its first baseball cards in 1951 and quickly became a fan favorite.

"FATHER OF BASEBALL"

Henry Chadwick did not invent baseball or even play it, but no one was more responsible for spreading the word about it. Starting out as a reporter in New York, he eventually wrote dozens of books on baseball, including the first hardcover book in 1868. He helped draft rule books and edited the annual guide to the National League. Of more interest to today's fans, he invented the box score (right) as well as the symbol-based scoring system used today.

FIRST THING IN THE MORNING

The first thing that many baseball fan turn to in the morning paper is the collection of box scores from games played the night before. Each game is summed up in a neat vertical box containing words, symbols, and numbers, explaining who won, who scored, who got how many hits, who pitched how many innings, even who the umpires were. This box score shows a 10-3 victory by the San Diego Padres over the St. Louis Cardinals.

KEEPING SCORE

Fans can follow the game by keeping score—that is, by using a recognized series of symbols and numbers to record the results of each batter throughout the game. This scorecard is from the 1932 World Series game in which Babe Ruth "called his shot."

HOW TO CALCULATE TWO IMPORTANT BASEBALL STATISTICS

Batting average:
Hits / At-Bats. Example:
$$\frac{125\ H}{435\ AB} = .287$$

Earned run average:
(Earned Runs x 9)/
Innings Pitched.
Example:
$$\frac{(62\ ER \times 9)}{251\ IP} = 2.22$$

Some sample symbols: K for strikeout; a dash for a single; 4-3 for a ground out, second to first

Vital statistics

Name and position, in this case, 1997 NL MVP Larry Walker of the Rockies

Final score

Team (visiting team on top)

Players listed in batting order, with position

Totals of each column of stats

The key stats: at-bats, runs, hits, runs batted in, walks, strikeouts, season batting average

McGwire's line shows two hits in four at-bats, with two RBI.

Line score shows runs by inning.

Padres 10, Cardinals 3

San Diego	AB	R	H	BI	BB	SO	Avg.
Veras 2b	4	2	0	0	1	1	.274
Gwynn rf	4	1	1	2	1	0	.316
RSanders lf	4	1	1	1	0	1	.298
Nevin 3b	5	1	1	0	0	0	.250
Joyner 1b	4	1	1	1	1	0	.250
Owens cf	4	2	2	0	0	0	.297
Hoffman p	1	0	1	0	2	0	.500
BDavis c	4	0	0	1	0	1	.304
Gomez ss	3	1	1	1	0	1	.240
Ashby p	2	0	1	0	0	0	.125
RRivera cf	1	1	1	0	0	0	.220
Totals	**36**	**10**	**10**	**9**	**5**	**2**	

St. Louis	AB	R	H	BI	BB	SO	Avg.
Drew cf	4	0	0	0	0	1	.261
McGee rf	4	0	0	0	0	1	.254
McGwire 1b	4	2	2	2	0	1	.279
Lankford lf	4	1	3	0	0	0	.307
Tatis 3b	3	0	1	1	0	1	.293
Renteria ss	4	0	0	0	1	1	.277
Paquette 2b	3	0	0	0	0	1	.333
Marrero c	1	0	0	0	0	0	.199
Luebbers p	0	0	0	0	0	0	.000
a-DHoward	1	0	0	0	0	0	.217
Acevedo p	0	0	0	0	0	0	.053
b-Polanco	0	0	0	0	0	0	.267
Mohler p	0	0	0	0	0	0	.000
Aybar p	0	0	0	0	0	0	.091
Totals	**32**	**3**	**6**	**3**	**3**	**4**	

San Diego	110 021 005—10 10 0
St. Louis	011 000 010— 3 6 3

a-walked for Luebbers in the 5th. b-grounded out for Acevedo in the 7th.
E—Renteria (19), Paquette (2), Marrero (5). **LOB**—San Diego 6, St. Louis 5. **2B**—Gwynn (14), Nevin (12), Hoffman (1), Lankford (21). **HR**—McGwire 2 (44) off Ashby 2. **RBIs**—Gwynn 2 (33), Nevin 2 (43), Joyner (31), Hoffman 2 (2), Gomez 2 (6), McGwire 2 (101), Renteria (44). **SB**—Veras (20), RSanders 2 (26), Owens 2 (26), Drew (9). **S**—Ashby. **SF**—Gomez. **GIDP**—Renteria.
Runners left in scoring position—San Diego 4 (RSanders 2, Joyner, BDavis); St. Louis 2 (McGee, Luebbers). **Runners moved up**—Nevin, BDavis, Paquette.
DP—San Diego 1 (Gomez, Veras and Joyner).

San Diego	IP	H	R	ER	BB	SO	NP	ERA
Ashby W, 10-5	7⅔	5	3	3	3	3	108	3.40
Hoffman S, 27	1⅓	1	0	0	0	1	19	2.89

St. Louis	IP	H	R	ER	BB	SO	NP	ERA
Luebbers L, 1-2	5	5	4	4	4	1	73	5.24
Acevedo	2	2	1	1	0	1	26	6.23
Mohler	1	0	0	0	0	0	15	4.89
Aybar	1	3	5	5	1	1	0	18	3.98

IBB—By Aybar (Joyner), by Ashby (Marrero). **U**—Nelson, Hirschbeck, Bell, Wegner. **T**—2:47. Tickets sold—45,106.

Various events in game are in bold.

Player who did it and new season total. This shows Gwynn with 2 RBI, for a season total of 33.

Pitcher's line scores: innings pitched, hits allowed, runs allowed, earned runs allowed, walks, strikeouts, number of pitches, and season earned-run average

---

LARRY WALKER RF — 13

HT: 6'3" WT: 225 BATS: L
BORN: 12/1/66
SIGNED THROUGH: 1998
RESIDES: AURORA, CO

1997	AB	HR	RBI
vs. Left	144	6	23
vs. Right	424	43	107
Home	302	20	68
Away	266	29	62
Day	261	25	73
Night	307	24	57
Grass	469	38	106
Turf	99	11	24
1st Half	309	25	68
2nd Half	259	24	62

1997	BA	OBA	SLG
vs. Left	.299	.400	.521
vs. Right	.389	.470	.788
Home	.384	.460	.709
Away	.346	.443	.733
Day	.414	.495	.835
Night	.326	.415	.622
Grass	.371	.457	.712
Turf	.343	.425	.758
1st Half	.388	.496	.741
2nd Half	.328	.391	.695

YR	TEAM	R	H	2B	3B	HR	TB	RBI	SB	OB%	SLG%	BA
1989	Expos	4	8	0	0	0	8	4	1	.264	.170	.170
1990	Expos	59	101	18	3	19	182	51	21	.326	.434	.241
1991	Expos	59	141	30	2	16	223	64	14	.349	.458	.290
1992	Expos	85	159	31	4	23	267	93	18	.353	.506	.301
1993	Expos	85	130	24	5	22	230	86	29	.371	.469	.265
1994	Expos	76	127	44	2	19	232	86	15	.394	.587	.322
1995	Rockies	96	151	31	5	36	300	101	16	.381	.607	.306
1996	Rockies	58	75	18	4	18	155	58	18	.342	.570	.276
1997	Rockies	143	208	46	4	49	409	130	33	.452	.720	.366
MLB TOTALS		665	1100	242	29	202	2006	673	165	.374	.542	.297

Larry not only enjoyed the first 40-homer campaign of his nine-year career in 1997 but emerged as a strong contender for the National League's MVP award. He finished with career peaks in numerous offensive categories. In addition to his slugging, Larry is also a good base runner and a fine right fielder whose arm is respected by runners.

1997 FIELDING STATISTICS

	G	GS	Inn.	PO	A	E	DP	Pct.	Rng.
Walker	150	143	1235.1	230	12	2	5	.992	1.76
RF Avg.	29	24	211.2	48	2	1	0	.977	2.11

Fielding stats

Stories and facts about the player

STATS HEAVEN

Although it sometimes features other information, the back of a player's baseball card usually contains a wealth of statistics. Often included are the player's lifetime batting or pitching statistics, listed year-by-year; an additional note in the text describing awards or special events; and the player's vital statistics, such as height, weight, and date of birth. Fans can quickly check a player's card for almost anything they might need to know.

Umpires' names

The minor leagues

This ball was used in play by the 1913 International League.

Bᴇꜰᴏʀᴇ ᴀ ᴘʟᴀʏᴇʀ ᴄᴀɴ ᴍᴀᴋᴇ ᴛʜᴇ "Sʜᴏᴡ," he's going to spend time on the "farm." That's a nickname for the minor leagues, which have been around since the 1870s. Starting in the 1920s, minor league teams created one-on-one relationships with Major League teams, building a system that funnels players up the chain into the big club. In the years following World War II, the minors reached their peak, with more than 400 teams playing in nearly 60 leagues. Today, 19 leagues include nearly 200 teams, most affiliated with Major League clubs. The "pyramid" of the minors moves from Rookie level, through Single, Double, and Triple A. For the most part, the teams are based in midsize cities or towns and bring a professional baseball product to fans far from the big-city lights. Those fans hope the players they watch there will someday move up to star in the Show.

HARDBALL NO MATTER WHERE YOU PLAY IT
The action on the field at minor league games is no less intense than it is in the big leagues—it just usually happens in front of fewer people. In fact, given that players are fighting for jobs, games can be even more fiercely fought. This home-plate action from a 2009 game between the Lincoln Saltdogs (sliding) and Wichita Wing Nuts looks like it could have happened at Fenway Park.

Catcher wears hockey-style helm that covers back the head.

WHERE THE LEGENDS BEGIN

Only a small handful of players go directly from high school or college to the big leagues. Even the greatest superstars spend time in the minor leagues, honing their talents and adjusting to a higher level of play. Below, Joe DiMaggio is shown at right as a member of the Pacific Coast League's San Francisco Seals. After batting .361 and putting together a 61-game hitting streak, DiMaggio moved on to the Yankees and eventually the Hall of Fame. Today, even a big star like Albert Pujols can look back to the time he spent with three minor league teams.

Martinez wore the same number in the minor leagues as he wears in the Majors.

SURPRISE GUESTS

Fans of minor league teams certainly root for the players they see every day. However, they sometimes get a great bonus: superstar Major League players working their way back from injury. For example, here's former Cy Young Award winner Pedro Martinez making a start in 2009 for the Lehigh Valley IronPigs before rejoining the Phillies following arm surgery. Another superstar who revisited the minors in 2009 was Manny Ramirez of the Los Angeles Dodgers . . . and the Albuquerque Isotopes!

WACKY NAMES

One of the ways that minor league teams try to attract fans is by using unusual names. While some clubs just mimic their big-league partners, others, such as the London Werewolves (cap shown at right), go another route. Witness the Dust Devils, Lake Monsters, Quakes, Isotopes, 51s, AquaSox, and Mud Hens, all real minor league teams.

SUMMER BASEBALL

Occupying a zone between college and the minors is the world of the National Baseball Congress. Started before World War II, the NBC was originally made up of "semipro" teams associated with towns or companies. Today, these have been replaced by amateur summer teams, filled mostly with college players working on their skills, along with former pros who just can't leave the game behind. Since 1935, the NBC's annual World Series has crowned a summer-ball champion, such as the Santa Barbara Foresters, shown here celebrating their championship in 2008.

A PIG OF A PITCHER

Costumed mascots are a staple of minor league games. Shown above is FeFe, the mascot for the IronPigs (*Fe* is the chemical symbol for iron). These characters interact with fans and players, take part in on-field skits and promotions, and appear at local events to help sell tickets.

International baseball

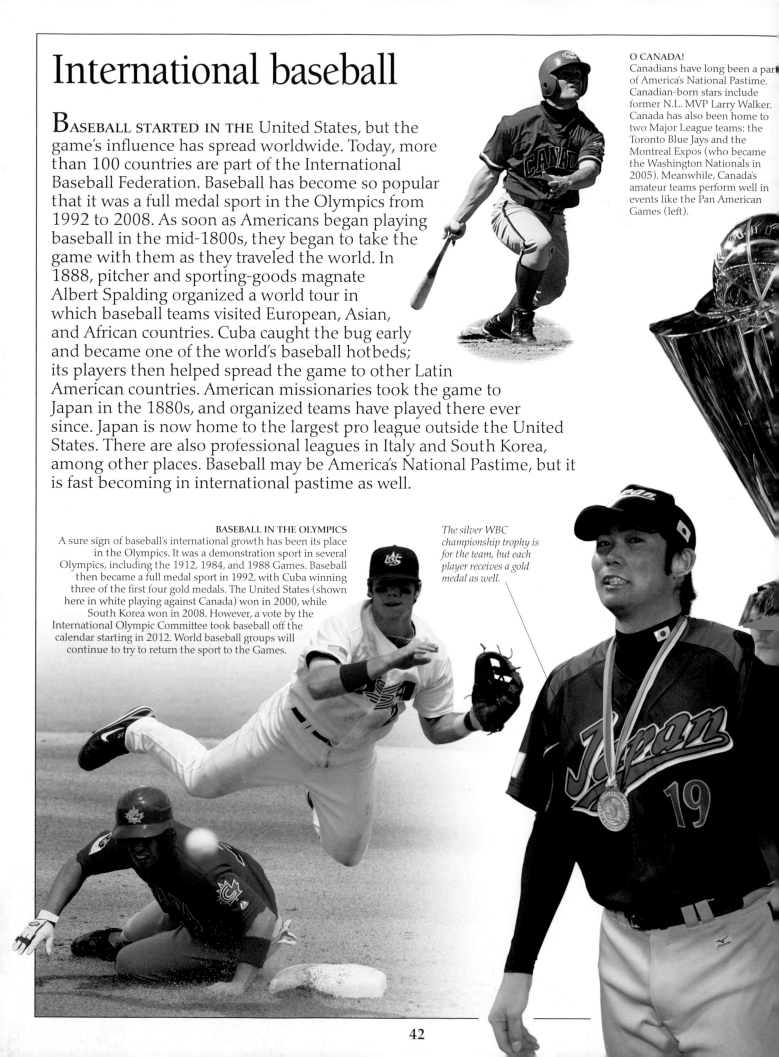

BASEBALL STARTED IN THE United States, but the game's influence has spread worldwide. Today, more than 100 countries are part of the International Baseball Federation. Baseball has become so popular that it was a full medal sport in the Olympics from 1992 to 2008. As soon as Americans began playing baseball in the mid-1800s, they began to take the game with them as they traveled the world. In 1888, pitcher and sporting-goods magnate Albert Spalding organized a world tour in which baseball teams visited European, Asian, and African countries. Cuba caught the bug early and became one of the world's baseball hotbeds; its players then helped spread the game to other Latin American countries. American missionaries took the game to Japan in the 1880s, and organized teams have played there ever since. Japan is now home to the largest pro league outside the United States. There are also professional leagues in Italy and South Korea, among other places. Baseball may be America's National Pastime, but it is fast becoming in international pastime as well.

O CANADA!
Canadians have long been a part of America's National Pastime. Canadian-born stars include former N.L. MVP Larry Walker. Canada has also been home to two Major League teams: the Toronto Blue Jays and the Montreal Expos (who became the Washington Nationals in 2005). Meanwhile, Canada's amateur teams perform well in events like the Pan American Games (left).

BASEBALL IN THE OLYMPICS
A sure sign of baseball's international growth has been its place in the Olympics. It was a demonstration sport in several Olympics, including the 1912, 1984, and 1988 Games. Baseball then became a full medal sport in 1992, with Cuba winning three of the first four gold medals. The United States (shown here in white playing against Canada) won in 2000, while South Korea won in 2008. However, a vote by the International Olympic Committee took baseball off the calendar starting in 2012. World baseball groups will continue to try to return the sport to the Games.

The silver WBC championship trophy is for the team, but each player receives a gold medal as well.

HOPE THEY'RE ALL GOOD CATCHERS

After winning the 2008 Japan Series, the Saitama Seibu Lions gave their manager, Hisanobu Watanabe, a celebratory toss. Japan has 12 pro teams in the Central and Pacific leagues that play a 130-game schedule in the spring and summer.

JAPAN'S YANKEES

Like the New York Yankees in America's Major Leagues, the Yomiuri Giants have dominated Japanese baseball for decades. The Giants are the most popular team; they're also the most successful, having won 32 championships since 1951, including a record nine in a row from 1965 to 1973. All-time home-run champion Sadaharu Oh starred for the Giants until 1980.

Yoshinobu Takahashi slugs a grand slam in the 1999 opener.

THE WORLD CHAMPS

In 2009, the national team from Japan once again hoisted the championship trophy at the World Baseball Classic. First held in 2006, this international tournament takes place in the spring, so that Major League players are available. Games are played in several nations, with the finals in the United States. So far, Japan, Korea, Cuba, and the U.S. have been among the top teams.

Uniform uses Mexican national colors of red and green.

VIVA MEXICO!

Since the 1930s, American pros have spent the winter in Mexico, improving their game against top competitors. A thriving pro league continues today, with national all-star teams (left) performing well at international tournaments. In addition, many Mexican-born players star in the Major Leagues, including pitchers Yovani Gallardo of the Milwaukee Brewers and Joakim Soria of the Kansas City Royals, a 2009 A.L. All-Star.

COUNTRY TO COUNTRY

The United States and Cuba maintain a decades-long diplomatic separation. But in the summer of 1999, the two countries got together on the baseball field. For the first time since the 1950s, a Major League team, the Baltimore Orioles, traveled to Havana to play the Cuban national team. In return, the Cubans played at Baltimore's Camden Yards. Before the first game, Orioles star Cal Ripken, Jr., and Cuban superstar Omar Linares enjoyed a little player-to-player international relations.

The Negro Leagues

FOR THE FIRST HALF OF THE 20TH CENTURY, Major League teams barred African-Americans from taking part. While such behavior would be scorned, not to mention illegal, today, the racist attitudes of the times allowed this discrimination to go on. But while black players could not play in the Major Leagues, nothing was going to stop them from playing the game. As early as the 1870s, all-black amateur teams were competing in the Northeast. By the turn of the century, black pro teams began to form, and leagues followed soon after. The "Negro Leagues," as they were known, included some of the greatest players of the century—players whose skills, most observers felt, would have made them Major League legends. The heyday of the Negro Leagues came in the 1930s and 1940s, when a dozen or so teams (including the Birmingham Black Barons, cap shown above) played to packed houses in major cities in the Northeast and Midwest. After 1947, when Jackie Robinson became the first black player in the Majors since the 19th century, the Negro Leagues slowly died out. Black players joined Major and minor league teams and took their rightful places at the highest level of the American game.

THE "BLACK BABE RUTH"

Of all the many outstanding players from the Negro Leagues, catcher Josh Gibson was perhaps greatest, and a batter of enormous strength. Unofficial records give him more than 900 home runs for his career. In 1931, he was credited with 75 home runs, while his career batting average was above .350. Major Leaguers of the time, including the great pitcher Walter Johnson, recognized Gibson's talents, but knew that he could never show them off on the big stage. In 1972, he became the second player elected to the Hall of Fame for his play in the Negro Leagues.

Before helmets, catchers wore their hats backward.

Gibson-autographed baseball

THE 42-YEAR-OLD ROOKIE

Leroy "Satchel" Paige was by far the most famous and successful player from the Negro Leagues. While his outstanding control as a pitcher first got him noticed, it was his infectious, cocky, and enthusiastic personality that made him a star. Paige once walked the bases loaded on purpose to face Josh Gibson. Then he struck the great catcher out. On tours of towns across America, Paige would have his fielders sit down behind him, and then strike out three batters in a row. In 1948 at the age of 42, he joined the Cleveland Indians and attracted record crowds at every game he pitched.

SATCHEL PAIGE'S own story

Pitchin' Man

TWENTY FIVE CENTS

As told to HAL LEBOVITZ

Book published after Paige joined the Indians

THE FASTEST MAN IN SPIKES
Satchel Paige, a teammate of James "Cool Papa" Bell, claimed that Bell was so fast "he could switch off the light and be in bed before the room got dark." Bell used his blinding speed and great batting stroke to star in the Negro Leagues from 1922 to 1950. He joined the Hall of Fame in 1974.

Paige was elected to the Baseball Hall of Fame in 1971.

Bell played for the Monarchs, Grays, Crawfords, and six other Negro League teams.

Baggy wool pants

TOP TEAMS
Along with the Homestead Grays, who won eight league pennants from 1937 to 1945, the Pittsburgh Crawfords (below) were among the Negro Leagues' greatest teams. Three of the four players pictured here—Oscar Charleston and Josh Gibson on the left and Judy Johnson on the right—are in the Baseball Hall of Fame. Charleston in particular combined speed, defense, and hitting at the highest level of skill. New York Giants manager John McGraw called him the best player in the game, black or white.

College baseball

FOR MOST OF BASEBALL'S FIRST 150 YEARS, college baseball existed in the background. Most players went right to the pros out of high school, and college teams didn't get the notice of Major or even minor league teams. In the early 20th century, in fact, "college men" were regarded as too "soft" for the rough-and-tumble sport. That feeling changed over the years, and today a larger portion of pros than ever come from the college ranks. Colleges at every level have teams, with the top teams earning national fame at the annual College World Series. Pro organizations watch the college circuit closely to find future stars. They choose players from college (and high school) in the annual amateur draft, held in June. College players are eligible after their junior seasons. They can also be drafted directly from two-year community colleges.

A COLLEGE MAN
Perhaps the first real college ballplayer to achieve national fame was pitcher Christy Mathewson. In a time when collegians were as rare as left-handed catchers, Mathewson went from Bucknell University to a Hall of Fame career.

LONGTIME HOME
The first College World Series was not played until 1947. In 1950, it was first played in Omaha, where has been held ever since. Today, th top teams from each of eight nation regions come to Omaha for a double elimination tournament. The game are played at cozy Rosenblatt Stadium, shown above. In 2011, the series will move to the new TD Ameritrade Park and Rosenblat will fade into history.

THE PING OF THE BAT
College baseball teams generally follow American League rules. However, there is one big difference: the bat. Since 1974, colleges (along with high-school and youth leagues) have used aluminum bats instead of wood. These bats are more expensive, but they are much harder to break and last much longer, thus saving money. Nevertheless, purists and safety advocates are working to reintroduce the wooden bat at all levels of play.

COLLEGE GAME ONE
These two baseballs were used in what is regarded as the first college baseball game, between Williams and Amherst in 1859. As agreed before the game, each team supplied the ball the other team would hit. The ball pitched by Amherst is on the right. They won 73-32.

COLLEGE STARS
By the 1970s, college baseball was starting to turn out a larger number of pros. Here are a trio of great examples. Robin Ventura (left) had a 58-game hitting streak with Oklahoma State and went on to a solid 16-year Major League career. Dave Winfield (center) helped the University of Minnesota reach the College World Series, then played 22 years in the Majors, cracking 3,110 hits, earning 12 All-Star selections, and making the Hall of Fame. Barry Bonds (right) was an Arizona State Sun Devil before he became a seven-time MVP and the single-season and career home-run champion.

College uniforms are similar to those in the Majors.

THE KING OF COLLEGE
University of Southern California coach Rod Dedeaux (right) won more College World Series championships than any other skipper. He and his Trojans racked up 11 titles from 1942 to 1986. Dozens of future Major Leaguers played for Dedeaux, who remained a big part of the game until his death in 2006. Standing to his left here is another future pro—Jack Del Rio played football, too, and enjoyed an 11-year career in the NFL.

Players from the bullpen and bench join players on the field for the celebratory dog pile.

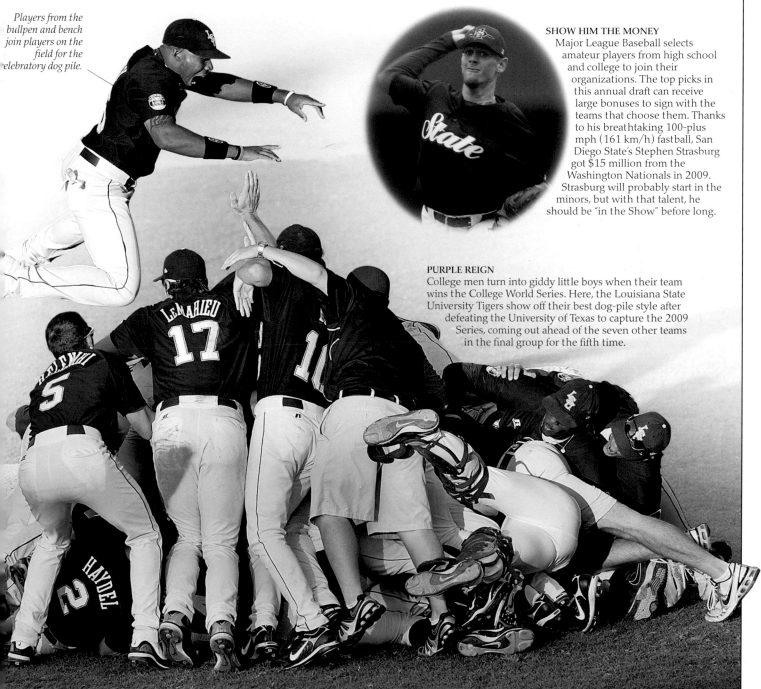

SHOW HIM THE MONEY
Major League Baseball selects amateur players from high school and college to join their organizations. The top picks in this annual draft can receive large bonuses to sign with the teams that choose them. Thanks to his breathtaking 100-plus mph (161 km/h) fastball, San Diego State's Stephen Strasburg got $15 million from the Washington Nationals in 2009. Strasburg will probably start in the minors, but with that talent, he should be "in the Show" before long.

PURPLE REIGN
College men turn into giddy little boys when their team wins the College World Series. Here, the Louisiana State University Tigers show off their best dog-pile style after defeating the University of Texas to capture the 2009 Series, coming out ahead of the seven other teams in the final group for the fifth time.

A kid's game

At least once every season, you hear a Major Leaguer say, "I sometimes can't believe it. I'm getting paid to play a kid's game." Although baseball didn't start with kids, kids are at the base of the game's support. Millions of boys and girls around the world play baseball, in organized leagues or with their friends in backyards and parks. Players at the highest levels do the same things they did when they were kids: hitting, pitching, and catching. Kids also are tremendous fans of baseball. Visit any Major League park and you'll see hundreds of kids cheering on their heroes or crowding around them afterward for autographs. Baseball may be a game for everyone, but deep down, it is a game for kids.

LITTLE KIDS . . . BIG-TIME ACTION
Kids play baseball with as much heart and excitement as their Major League heroes. This action at the plate from the 2009 Little League World Series (won by a team from the United States) looks as if it could have come from a big-league game.

WE LOVE JUSTIN
These kids at a Minnesota Twins game are showing their love of their favorite player, Twins first baseman Justin Morneau. Wearing team gear "just like the pros" is a big deal for young fans, and one of many ways that they can show their loyalty.

Team logo

Baseball cap

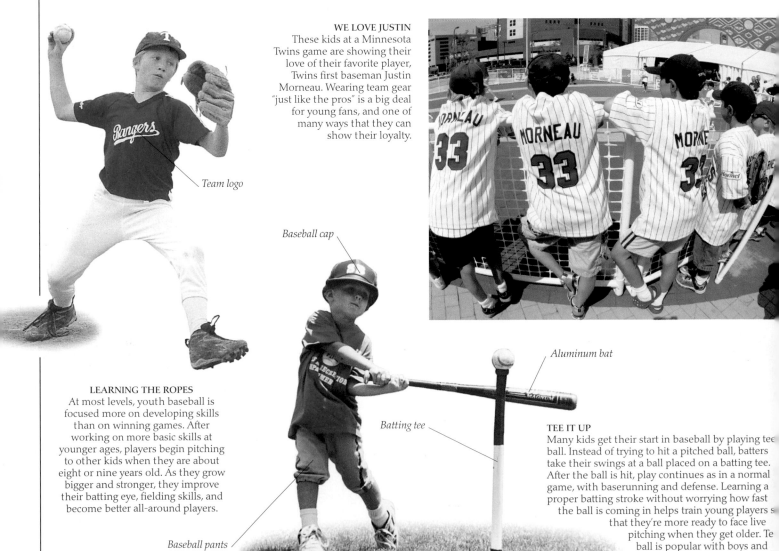

LEARNING THE ROPES
At most levels, youth baseball is focused more on developing skills than on winning games. After working on more basic skills at younger ages, players begin pitching to other kids when they are about eight or nine years old. As they grow bigger and stronger, they improve their batting eye, fielding skills, and become better all-around players.

Batting tee

Aluminum bat

Baseball pants

TEE IT UP
Many kids get their start in baseball by playing tee ball. Instead of trying to hit a pitched ball, batters take their swings at a ball placed on a batting tee. After the ball is hit, play continues as in a normal game, with baserunning and defense. Learning a proper batting stroke without worrying how fast the ball is coming in helps train young players s that they're more ready to face live pitching when they get older. Te ball is popular with boys and girls, from ages four to eight.

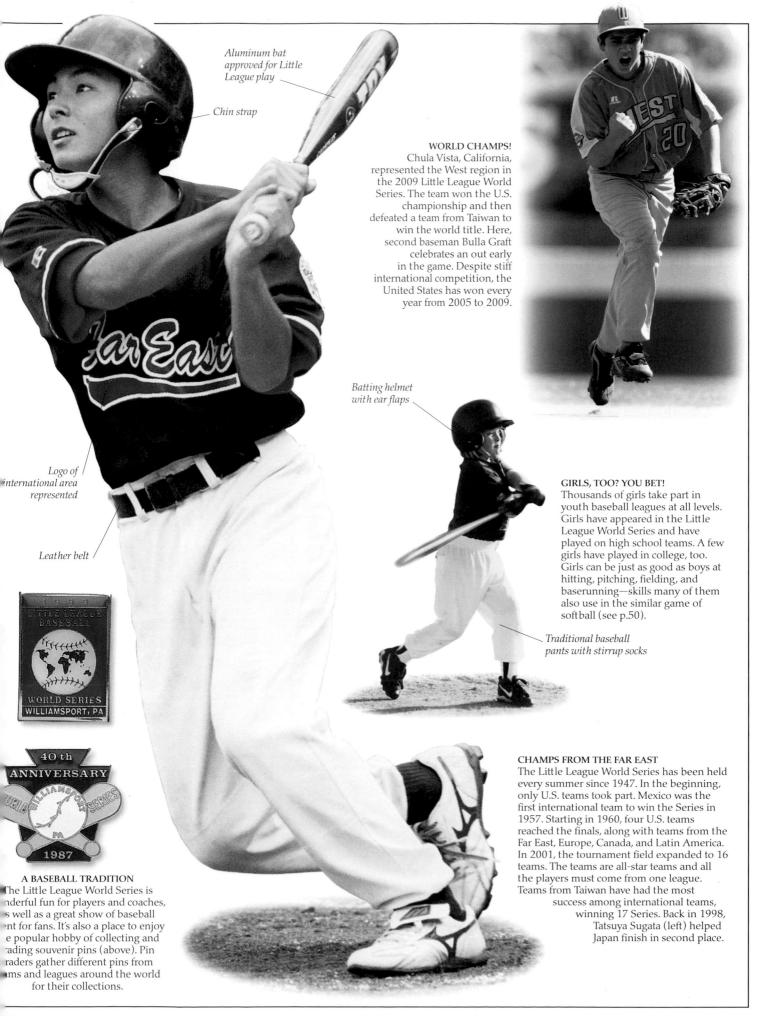

Aluminum bat approved for Little League play

Chin strap

WORLD CHAMPS!
Chula Vista, California, represented the West region in the 2009 Little League World Series. The team won the U.S. championship and then defeated a team from Taiwan to win the world title. Here, second baseman Bulla Graft celebrates an out early in the game. Despite stiff international competition, the United States has won every year from 2005 to 2009.

Batting helmet with ear flaps

Logo of international area represented

Leather belt

GIRLS, TOO? YOU BET!
Thousands of girls take part in youth baseball leagues at all levels. Girls have appeared in the Little League World Series and have played on high school teams. A few girls have played in college, too. Girls can be just as good as boys at hitting, pitching, fielding, and baserunning—skills many of them also use in the similar game of softball (see p.50).

Traditional baseball pants with stirrup socks

CHAMPS FROM THE FAR EAST
The Little League World Series has been held every summer since 1947. In the beginning, only U.S. teams took part. Mexico was the first international team to win the Series in 1957. Starting in 1960, four U.S. teams reached the finals, along with teams from the Far East, Europe, Canada, and Latin America. In 2001, the tournament field expanded to 16 teams. The teams are all-star teams and all the players must come from one league. Teams from Taiwan have had the most success among international teams, winning 17 Series. Back in 1998, Tatsuya Sugata (left) helped Japan finish in second place.

A BASEBALL TRADITION
The Little League World Series is wonderful fun for players and coaches, as well as a great show of baseball talent for fans. It's also a place to enjoy the popular hobby of collecting and trading souvenir pins (above). Pin traders gather different pins from teams and leagues around the world for their collections.

Women in baseball

No woman has ever played in a Major League game. But that has not stopped millions of women and girls from taking part in baseball. Many little girls start out in tee ball, but the most popular way to the game is softball, a form of baseball played on a smaller diamond with a bigger ball. Women and girls usually play fast-pitch softball, in which the ball is thrown underhand almost as fast as boys throw overhand. In the United States, there are women's pro softball leagues, and many foreign countries send women's teams to play Olympic softball. Young girls also play in organized baseball leagues, including Little League and Pony League groups. Since 1984, several girls have even appeared in the Little League World Series. Women also work as umpires and coaches in youth leagues.

MAKING A PITCH FOR WOMEN

Although Japanese baseball is still a male-dominated sport, Eri Yoshida is working to change that. In 2009, she made her debut as a knuckleballing relief pitcher with the minor league team Kobe 9 Cruise. She's only 17 and still in high school, but she learned to throw her pro-grade knuckler by watching Boston Red Sox pitcher Tim Wakefield.

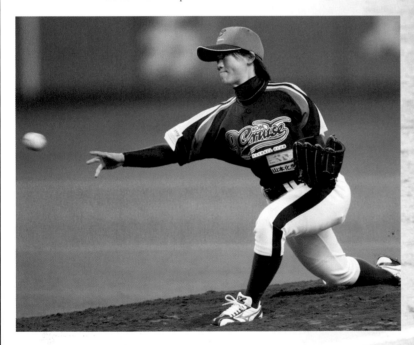

SOFTBALL SUPERSTARS

Fast-pitch softball is one way that many women take part in a sport much like baseball. Pitchers, such as Jennie Finch, who led the U.S. team to the 2004 Olympic gold medal, throw underhand at speeds reaching 80 miles per hour (129 km/h). In softball, the bases are only 60 feet (18 m) apart, as opposed to 90 (27 m). The ball is about 40 percent bigger than a baseball, but is not, as the name of the sport implies, soft. Beyond that, softball at this level and baseball are much the same, with outs, strikes, balls, innings, and runs. Pitching is more dominant in softball, however, since the mound is only 43 feet (13 m) from home plate; thus, scores are usually lower. Although young girls may play youth baseball, most play in organized softball leagues. High schools and colleges have fast-pitch softball programs, too.

First baseman's glove

Long-sleeved shirt

AAGBL players wore skirts.

Knee socks

STARS OF THE SILVER SCREEN
Interest in the AAGBL grew in the 1980s when former players began lobbying to have more of the history of the league included in the Hall of Fame. Their campaign helped push development of the movie *A League of Their Own*, which featured the Rockford Peaches.

Same type of glove as male players

A LEAGUE OF THEIR OWN
In 1943, with the Major Leagues depleted due to World War II, Chicago Cubs owner Philip Wrigley started a professional women's softball league to drum up fan interest. The league began play that year in South Bend, Indiana; Racine, Wisconsin; Rockford, Illinois; and Kenosha, Wisconsin. Nearly 200,000 fans came out to watch the games, and attendance increased a few years later when the league switched from playing softball (and pitching underhand) to playing baseball, changing their name to the All-American Girls Baseball League (AAGBL) as a result.

MORE TEAMS COME TO PLAY
The growth of the AAGBL continued after World War II. The Peoria Redwings joined the AAGBL in 1946 and played each season until 1951. The small midwestern city of Peoria, Illinois, was typical of the hometowns of the league's teams. The teams relied on support from small communities and avoided big-league competition.

PEORIA ILL.

BORDERS CRACKS THE BARRIER
In 1994, left-handed pitcher Ila Borders, the MVP of her high-school team, became the first woman to win a college baseball game. She played three years at Southern California College and one at Whittier. In 1997, the publicity-minded St. Paul Saints of the independent Northern League signed Borders to a pro contract, where she became one of the first women to start and win a professional baseball game. Borders also later played for the Duluth-Superior Dukes. Her success helped spur the short-lived Ladies League Baseball in 1997 and the traveling Colorado Silver Bullets team in 1997-98. Women still do not have a major place in professional baseball, but it's not for lack of trying.

Jerseys styled after women's blouses

Team logo on cap

All the managers were male.

ANYTHING FOR PUBLICITY
By 1948, the AAGBL had 10 teams in midwestern towns and cities; nearly one million fans attended games. Former Major League stars such as Jimmie Foxx and Max Carey were hired to manage the teams. And while much of the publicity surrounding the league focused on the novelty of female players, the women also gained respect for their skills on the diamond. Unfortunately, with Major Leaguers returning from the war, interest in the women's league began to die out. The AAGBL played its final season in 1954.

Ballparks

POETS HAVE WRITTEN about ballparks. Songs are composed in their honor. The brilliant green grass, the contrasting brown infield, the pastoral nature of the ball yard—all evoke feelings one doesn't get from a basketball arena or gigantic football stadium. The thrill baseball fans get from that first glimpse of green as they walk through a tunnel toward their seats is unlike any other in sports. Today, fathers, mothers, sons, and daughters continue to take that walk together, just as parents and children have for decades. Even today, as new parks spring up across the country, they are often designed to feel like old ballparks. With the sense of history that baseball creates, a ballpark is more than just a place where two teams play; it is, as the movie said, a field of dreams.

Christy Mathewson

FAN FOR FANS
From handheld fans honoring baseball heroes to pins made for Mother's Day (far left), there have been promotional items created for visitors as long as there have been ballparks. Now, special days are held throughout the season, when fans can get everything from bats to beach towels to bobblehead dolls.

THE SEAT WHERE THEY LIVED
This is a bleacher seat from Crosley Field, home of the Cincinnati Reds from 1912 to 1970. The fabled old field was demolished in 1970, after which the Reds moved to the more modern, but less charming Riverfront Stadium. The team now plays at the Great American Ballpark.

Usher's cap and ID pin

HOME OF "DA BUMS"
Few places have ever had a closer relationship to a ballpark than Brooklyn, New York, had to Ebbets Field. The tiny bandbox of a stadium was home to the Dodgers from 1913 to 1957, after which the team broke millions of local hearts and moved to Los Angeles. On the right field fence, clothier Abe Stark posted a billboard that read, "Hit Sign, Win Suit."

Outfield bleachers

Upper deck
Box seats

RETIRED NUMBERS
Most ballparks have a display of the team's retired numbers, such as this one at Yankee Stadium. Retired numbers honor great players and managers. No future players will wear those numbers for that team. Note the 42: All Major League teams retired that number in 1997 to honor racial barrier-breaker Jackie Robinson.

FRIENDLY CONFINES
One of baseball's most revered ballparks is Wrigley Field, home of the Chicago Cubs. Ivy (right) grows on its brick outfield walls. Clever fans often watch games from the roofs of the apartment buildings located behind the stadium.

Distance in feet from home plate

NO MORE RAIN DELAYS
Miller Park in Milwaukee joins several other newer ballparks in having a unique feature: a retractable roof. When weather threatens to delay a game, the roof can roll closed on a series of tracks to cover the entire field and the stands. Toronto's Skydome (now known as Rogers Centre) was the first sports stadium with this kind of roof.

A COZY LITTLE PARK
This aerial view of Tiger Stadium in Detroit shows how the park was squeezed into the neighborhood. This was how most early ballparks were constructed. Compare the cramped feeling of this old ball yard, built in 1912, with the expansive design of Cleveland's Progressive Field (below). The Tigers played their last game on this field in 1999, moving to Comerica Park for the 2000 season. Some fans bemoan the loss of these old ballparks. (Boston's Fenway Park is now the oldest park in the Majors. It, too, opened in 1912.) And while most people now agree that vast, impersonal stadiums are not the answer, fans have come out in droves to new stadiums in Baltimore, Pittsburgh, Minneapolis, and elsewhere. Why? Because they combine modern amenities with the best features of the old-time parks.

Scoreboard

Light tower

PROGRAMS! GET YOUR PROGRAMS!
Few fans leave a ballpark empty-handed. Concession stands, such as this one at Baltimore's Camden Yards, are located throughout the stadium and offer everything a fan could want.

TAKE US OUT TO THE BALLPARK
This panoramic view of Progressive Field in Cleveland shows how most baseball stadiums are laid out. A horseshoe of seats surrounds the field, with the bottom of the U-shape at home plate. Raised bleachers rise up beyond the outfield walls. Most fans think the best seats are behind home plate or along the baselines between the bases and home plate. But some fans swear by the cozy—and affordable—bleachers.

The Baseball Hall of Fame

Visiting the Baseball Hall of Fame is like taking a walk through a history book. Located in Cooperstown, New York, the Hall of Fame contains all of the important artifacts and memorabilia from baseball's past—with more items added every year. On display at the Hall are bats used by Nap Lajoie, Babe Ruth, and George Brett; balls hit by Lou Gehrig, Hank Aaron, and Albert Pujols; caps worn by Christy Mathewson, Satchel Paige, and Mark Buehrle; bases stolen by Ty Cobb, Lou Brock, and Rickey Henderson. There are also thousands of programs, scorecards, posters, pennants, and souvenirs to look at. The Hall's library contains millions of photographs and important baseball records, and serves as a key resource for scholars researching the sport. The most important function of the Hall of Fame, however, is to honor the greatest players, coaches, and contributors in the game. Each year, another class of baseball greats is inducted into the Hall, to remain forever a vital part of baseball's ongoing story.

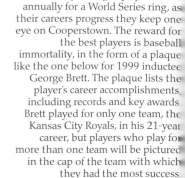

ULTIMATE HONOR
While Major League players strive annually for a World Series ring, as their careers progress they keep one eye on Cooperstown. The reward for the best players is baseball immortality, in the form of a plaque like the one below for 1999 inductee George Brett. The plaque lists the player's career accomplishments, including records and key awards. Brett played for only one team, the Kansas City Royals, in his 21-year career, but players who play for more than one team will be pictured in the cap of the team with which they had the most success.

THE RYAN EXPRESS
Nolan Ryan pitched in the Major Leagues for 27 seasons, the most of any player. His overpowering fastball made him dominant for many of those years. He is the all-time career leader in strikeouts, and set the modern single-season record in 1973 with a total of 383. Ryan also threw seven no-hitters, the most by any pitcher. The ball above is now on display at the Hall of Fame, where Ryan was inducted in 1999.

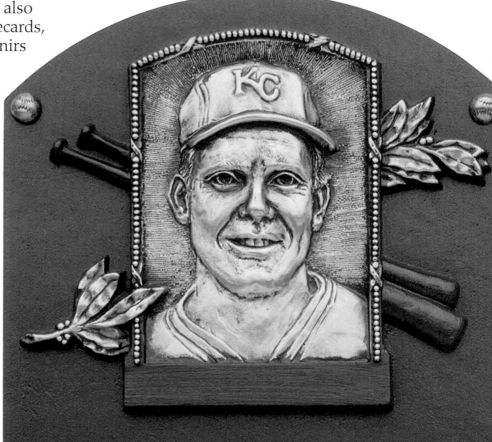

GEORGE HOWARD BRETT
KANSAS CITY, A.L., 1973 – 1993

PLAYED EACH GAME WITH CEASELESS INTENSITY AND UNBRIDLED PASSION LIFETIME MARKS INCLUDE .305 BA, 317 HR, 1,595 RBI AND 3,154 HITS ELEVEN .300 SEASONS. A 13-TIME ALL-STAR AND THE FIRST PLAYER TO WIN BATTING TITLES IN THREE DECADES (1976, '80, '90). HIT .390 IN 1980 MVP SEASON AND LED ROYALS TO FIRST WORLD SERIES TITLE IN 1985. RANKS AMONG ALL-TIME LEADERS IN HITS, DOUBLES, LONG HITS AND TOTAL BASES. A.L. CAREER RECORD, MOST INTENTIONAL WALKS. A CLUTCH HITTER WHOSE PROFOUND RESPECT FOR THE GAME LED TO UNIVERSAL REVERENCE.

Honus Wagner — Grover Cleveland Alexander — Tris Speaker — Napoleon Lajoie — George Sisler — Walter Johnson

Eddie Collins | Babe Ruth | Connie Mack | Cy Young

A GATHERING OF GREATNESS
In 1936, baseball began electing players and coaches to the Baseball Hall of Fame. The Hall itself didn't open until 1939, on the alleged 100th anniversary of baseball (the anniversary was based on the now-debunked theory that Abner Doubleday "invented" the game in 1839). This photograph of nearly all the then-living Hall of Fame members was taken at the dedication. Ty Cobb was also at the event, but missed the photograph.

B for Brooklyn

JACKIE'S CAP
The Hall of Fame boasts an enormous collection of baseball caps, including this one worn by Dodgers great Jackie Robinson. The collection includes caps from every era of pro and amateur baseball. When asked, players gladly donate their caps to the Hall to commemorate a special occasion.

Classic Yankee pinstripes

TICKET TO HISTORY
This 1956 World Series ticket is an example of the Hall of Fame's vast resources on the paper record of baseball. Each season, the historians at the Hall add many more items to their collection of tickets, scorebooks, magazines, books, and newspaper articles.

MAGIC MITT
The Hall of Fame is a great place to compare old-time gear, such as this 1950s catcher's mitt used by Roy Campanella, with today's more high-tech baseball tools.

DIRTY DIMAGGIO
One of the great hallmarks of the artifacts fans can see at the Hall of Fame is their authenticity. This jersey is one example. Worn by Yankee great Joe DiMaggio, it retains the sweat, dirt, and grass stains that the "Yankee Clipper" put there himself. The artifacts aren't replicas—they're the real McCoy. Along with the hundreds of items on display, the Hall also carefully stores and preserves thousands of other pieces of baseball memorabilia, creating new exhibits each season that highlight different aspects of baseball's past.

WELCOME TO THE HALL!
The annual Hall of Fame induction ceremony is one of the greatest events of each baseball season. Inductees are presented in front of a crowd of thousands and give speeches broadcast nationwide thanking those who helped them reach the top. Shown here are speedster Rickey Henderson and slugger Jim Rice as they were inducted in July 2009.

Spring training

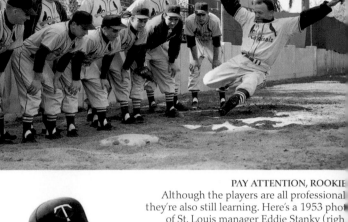

AFTER A LONG WINTER, the arrival of spring means baseball is back! Since the 1920s, teams have headed to Florida to prepare for the upcoming season; starting in the 1940s, Arizona has been a destination, too. What do they do there? They train—that's why they call it spring training. Teams look at young players, veterans prepare for the new season, and managers and coaches organize their strategies. In the early days, players had offseason jobs, so they used spring training to prepare their bodies for play. These days, players come to "camp" ready to play. For fans, spring training is a great way to see their heroes up-close in smaller, more casual settings.

PAY ATTENTION, ROOKIE
Although the players are all professional they're also still learning. Here's a 1953 photo of St. Louis manager Eddie Stanky (right) demonstrating good sliding technique to flock of Cardinals rookie

Players wear batting-practice jerseys without numbers during warmups.

WORKING ON SKILLS
During the regular season, Joe Crede is a slugging infielder with the Minnesota Twins, but at spring training he's just another player working on the full set of the baseball skills. Crede might not have many chances to bunt during the season, but in spring he works on this important technique. Spring training's many hours on the diamond give players a chance to perfect every aspect of their game.

SUPERSTAR TAN
Of course, when you're a baseball superstar, you might not have to spend as much time working on your skills. Here's Hall of Famer Ted Williams working on his tan during spring training in sunny Florida in 1949. Then as now, stars of Williams' caliber can use spring training as a nice mini-vacation before the grind of the regular season starts.

ONE MORE QUESTION
The more casual atmosphere at spring training means players have a little more time to spend with the media answering questions. Here's Yankees superstar Derek Jeter (in cap) fielding questions from a pack of reporters. During spring training, these reporters can get more time with the players than they'll be able to get once the season starts. Players also pose for team and baseball-card photos, and film commercials and promotional spots for the upcoming season.

SPRING HOMES
Baseball teams need good weather to play their spring games and hold their practice sessions. Florida and Arizona provide great weather and short distances between ballparks, making them perfect homes for teams and players preparing for the season. These pins commemorate spring training sessions in each of the two locales.

WHATEVER WORKS

[Eve]ry Major League team has a large staff of trainers who [wo]rk with players to make sure they're in great shape. In [rec]ent years, teams have found many new ways of working [o]ut. Here, Ronny Paulino of the Philadelphia Phillies [st]retches with a medicine ball. Spring training is a great [tim]e to introduce new workout routines, such as yoga, that [giv]e players more ways to stay healthy during the season.

WORKING HARD

Even when you win the A.L. MVP, you still work during spring training. Here's Red Sox second baseman Dustin Pedroia doing wind sprints. The drag chute he's wearing makes the running harder and helps him build the endurance he'll need to play 162 games.

TIME TO PLAY

Teams play a full schedule of games during spring training. In Florida, participating teams play in the Grapefruit League. In Arizona, it's the Cactus League. This Cactus League action between the San Francisco Giants (top) and Arizona Diamondbacks shows that although the games don't really count, that doesn't mean the players don't go all out. Managers and coaches use the games to test lineups, see new players and pitchers, and try out new strategies. Fans love the games because the seats are closer and the ticket prices are much less than they'd pay in the regular season.

By using a pop-up slide, Justin Upton can quickly get up and run home after third baseman Pedro Sandoval misses the ball.

MEETING THEIR HEROES

The easygoing atmosphere at spring training means that players, such as the Yankees' Hideki Matsui (left), are more available for autographs than they are during the regular season. Fans flock to ballparks in Florida and Arizona for an up-close meeting with today's stars and tomorrow's heroes.

57

World Series history

Note early spelling of "base ball."

THE HISTORY OF Major League Baseball can be traced almost completely by following the timeline of the World Series. The game's annual championship—played between the champions of the American and National Leagues—has become as much a part of America's calendar as the Fourth of July. The first Fall Classic, as it is sometimes called, was in 1903 (left), and it has been played every year—with one notable exception—since 1905. The exception? The 1994 World Series was canceled during a labor dispute between players and owners. Every other year, the World Series has gone on through war and peace and everything in between. While generations of baseball's greatest players have created indelible memories on the field (see p. 60), the constant popularity of the World Series has helped create a colorful legacy of Series stuff, as shown on these pages.

THE BLACK SOX
The fan who used this ticket to the 1919 World Series between the Cincinnati Reds and the Chicago White Sox witnessed one of baseball's darkest hours. Eight members of the White Sox conspired with gamblers to throw the Series to the underdog Reds. The "Black Sox," as they came to be known, were later suspended from baseball for life. One of them, "Shoeless" Joe Jackson, was one of the greatest hitters of all time. There is debate about Jackson's role in the fix, but there is no debate that the fix was in. Baseball's pure reputation had been tarnished.

An early version of the event's name

Even ba then, t Series w used sell goo

PINNING DOWN THE WORLD SERIES

The now-popular hobby of collecting pins commemorating major sports events did not start with the Olympics. Pins such as the ones below have been issued for the World Series since the first games. An example from 1913 (bottom right) shows an early version of the name of the event: "World's Series." The members of the press covering the Series have always enjoyed special pins, such as the ribbon in the center, issued in 1917 by the New York Giants, and the pin at upper left, issued by the American League in 1927.

Pin from 1908, the year of the Giants' first Series

Note low $5 price for a great seat.

New York Giants tie tack

Baseball premade for canceled 1994 Series

THE SERIES THAT WASN'T

Disagreements between owners and players have been a part of baseball since the 1860s. The worst example of baseball labor problems came in 1994. Amid an ongoing battle over salaries, the players went on strike on August 12, and they didn't return until 1995. For the only time since 1905, the World Series was canceled.

BOSTON AND THE BABE

The great Babe Ruth first made an impact on the World Series in 1916, making his mark as a pitcher, not a hitter. Ruth's 14-inning, complete game, one-run victory in Game 2 proved to be the key to Boston's title. The Red Sox would win again with Ruth in 1918 for their fifth title in 16 seasons. Ruth left two seasons later, and Boston didn't win again until 2004.

THE RIVALRY

For decades, the Brooklyn Dodgers and New York Yankees were fierce crosstown rivals, facing each other seven times in the World Series; Brooklyn won only in 1955. The Dodgers moved to Los Angeles in 1958, and in 1963, they swept the Yankees in the Series, winning in L.A. on the strength of pitcher Sandy Koufax's magical left arm.

Pennants representing
each Major League team

GODZILLA'S MONSTER MASH
In 2009, Hideki "Godzilla" Matsui, shown here hitting a Game 6 homer, became the first full-time designated hitter to be named World Series MVP. He hit .615 with 8 RBI, including a record-tying six in Game 6.

CHAMPAGNE DREAMS COME TRUE
At left, Andy Pettite of the Yankees proudly hoists the 2009 Commissioner's Trophy after his team's World Series victory. After the final game of each Series, the commissioner of baseball presents the trophy to the winning team's owners. Although the ceremony used to happen in the locker room, it now takes place on a stage hastily built on the field amid the celebrating players. What was once a champagne-soaked party in cramped, plastic-covered quarters has now become a field-spanning spectacle of fireworks, frivolity, and fun.

Newly printed Yankees
championship T-shirt, given
out to players on field

THE MIGHTY YANKEES
The New York Yankees have dominated the World Series like no other team. The Bronx Bombers have appeared in 40 World Series and won 27 times, more than twice as many as their nearest rivals, the Athletics and Cardinals. The Yankees won their first World Series in 1923. Their most recent victory was in 2009. This pennant is from their 1998 win. They are the only team to win four World Series in a row (1936–39), and also the only team to win five in a row (1949–53).

RINGING IN THE TITLE
While the World Series trophy resides in the winning team's offices, the players' symbol of victory is the World Series ring. This model, from the 1954 New York Giants, shows an early design. Recent rings are enormous, with many diamonds.

Yankees' famous
top hat logo

SOX SOUVENIR
Long-suffering Red Sox fans rejoiced when their team won the 2004 World Series. This bobblehead doll shows Manny Ramirez holding his Series MVP trophy.

World Series heroes

Two outs, bottom of the ninth, seventh game of the World Series. Your team is behind, and it's all up to you. Can you save the day? For more than 100 years, kids across America have played that scene in their heads and in their schoolyard games. Can you make the big hit and win the Series? Can you be a hero? When it came time for the men on these pages to ask that question of themselves, to face the great pressure of the World Series—whether bottom of the ninth or earlier—they all answered, "Yes, I can!" For these grown-up kids, it was a dream come true.

A-MAZ-ING
Until 1960, no team had earned its World Series title by hitting a home run on the final swing of the Series. Then along came Bill Mazeroski. The Pirates' second baseman, known more for his outstanding fielding than his hitting, led off the bottom of the ninth with the Yankees and Pirates tied 9-9 in Game 7. Maz slugged a home run over the left-field wall for a shocking 10-9 victory over the Yankees.

PITCHER PERFECT
On baseball's biggest stage, no pitcher was ever better for one game than Don Larsen. In the fifth game of the 1956 World Series, the Yankees right-hander threw the only perfect game in World Series history, and one of only 18 such games in all of baseball since 1880. Larsen, here being congratulated by catcher Yogi Berra, faced 27 Brooklyn Dodgers and retired them all. Not one Dodger reached first base.

Larsen's career record was 81-91.

THE YANKEE CLIPPER
Yankees center fielder Joe DiMaggio never won a World Series with a homer or made a Series-winning catch. He just won. In 13 seasons (1936–42 and 1946–51) with the Yankees, DiMaggio led the team to nine World Series titles. His clutch hitting (he had 30 RBI in 51 games), graceful fielding, and quiet leadership were the keystones to the great Yankees teams of the 1930s and 1940s. DiMaggio, who died in 1999, became an enduring symbol of the Yankees' dynasty.

GIMPY GIBBY
Although it came in Game 1 of the 1988 World Series, not Game 7, a dramatic two-run homer by injured and limping Kirk Gibson in the bottom of the ninth gave the Los Angeles Dodgers the lift they needed to upset the favored Oakland A's for the Series title.

A GREAT MAN ON AND OFF THE FIELD
In the 1971 World Series, Roberto Clemente, the pride of Puerto Rico, hit .414 while reaching base safely in all seven games. He had a key home run in Game 7 as the Pirates defeated the Orioles 2-1 to win the Series. Clemente's final Series appearance was bittersweet. Following the 1972 season, when he reached 3,000 career hits in his last game, Clemente was tragically killed in a plane crash while helping deliver supplies to earthquake victims in Nicaragua.

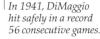

In 1941, DiMaggio hit safely in a record 56 consecutive games.

Jackson is fifth all-time with 10 career Series home runs.

FIVE FOR PHILLY
In the 2009 World Series, Philadelphia second baseman Chase Utley matched Reggie Jackson's record of five homers in a single Series. Utley's power was not enough to give the Phillies their second straight Series, however, and they lost to the Yankees in six games.

MISTER OCTOBER
Few players in baseball history have craved the limelight like Reginald Martinez Jackson. Reggie Jackson earned his nickname of "Mister October" with a string of clutch hits in World Series games for Oakland and New York. But it was in Game 6 of the 1977 World Series that he carved a permanent place in baseball lore. Jackson blasted home runs on three consecutive pitches from Dodgers hurlers. (Only Babe Ruth, who did it twice, has also hit three homers in a Series game.) He also set an all-time record by hitting a total of five home runs in that year's Series.

Fisk's bat

FISK AND FENWAY
Red Sox catcher Carlton Fisk ended what many call the greatest game in Series history—Game 6 in 1975—with a home run in the bottom of the 12th inning. Fisk's homer over Fenway Park's "Green Monster" gave Boston a 7-6 victory.

Jackson had 563 career home runs.

The home run

FOUR-BAGGER. Circuit clout. Round-tripper. Dinger. Tater. *Cuadrangular*. Homer. By any name, the home run is baseball's signature moment. Sock the ball out of the yard and you render the other team helpless. There is no defense for a home run. And nothing energizes a crowd or a team like a well-timed shot to the seats. All of baseball's greatest heroes are home-run hitters. The Babe. Larrupin' Lou. Old Double X. The Mick. Say-Hey Willie. Hammerin' Hank. Big Mac. The frenzy created by Mark McGwire, Sammy Sosa, and Barry Bonds as they chased home-run records wouldn't have happened if they had been chasing the marks for doubles. Unfortunately, news has come out since then that some players were probably breaking the rules (and the law) by using drugs that made them stronger—and some people believe that their home run records shouldn't stand. But even with the cloud over the record books, homers are exciting. Backbackbackback! Going, going, gone! Good-bye, Mr. Spalding! It might be, it could be, it is . . . a home run!

Aaron broke in with the Milwaukee Braves, who later moved to Atlanta.

HAMMERIN' HANK
On April 8, 1974, Hank Aaron broke a record many thought was unbreakable. The Braves outfielder, shown here early in his career, hit his 715th career home run, breaking the mark set by the immortal Babe Ruth. Aaron, who finished his career in 1976 with 755 homers, suffered through racist threats as he approached Ruth's record. But his class and talent overcame the bigotry. Sadly, Aaron remains one of the sports world's least appreciated superstars.

Sports Illustrated
715

No words were needed when Aaron set the record.

THE SHOT HEARD 'ROUND THE WORLD
Giants outfielder Bobby Thomson hit one of baseball's most famous home runs, a three-run shot in the bottom of the ninth that gave the Giants the 1951 National League championship over the Brooklyn Dodgers.

Thomson earned a hug from Giants manager Leo Durocher (left).

Compare the baggy pants worn by Aaron in 1961 with the sleek outfits of Bonds and Howard (right).

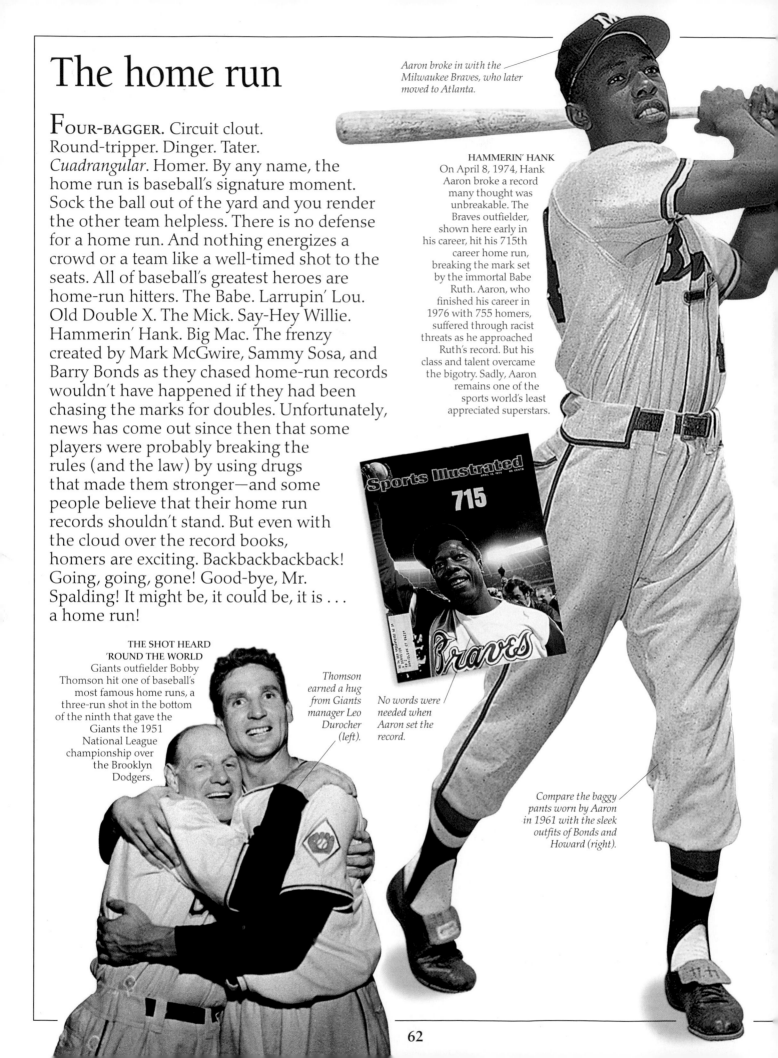

GOING FOR 61 IN '61

In 1961, Yankee outfielders Mickey Mantle and Roger Maris made a paired assault on Ruth's single-season home-run record of 60. Maris became the new home-run king with his 61st homer in the final game of the season, setting a mark that lasted until 1998.

The pressure of the assault on 60 caused Maris's hair to fall out.

A September 1961 hip injury ended Mantle's chase.

A DAY TO REMEMBER!

ROGER MARIS

THE MIGHTY MICK

With 536 home runs, Mickey Mantle is first all-time among switch-hitters, showing his power from both sides of the plate. But there is more to Mantle's home-run story than a number. He holds the career record for World Series home runs with 18, hitting them when his team needed them most. And he hit what has been called the longest home run ever, a mammoth 565-foot (172 m) blast in 1953 in Washington's Griffith Stadium. If not for his constant injury problems, Mantle might have caught the Babe, too.

Mantle underwent several knee surgeries.

Mantle's speed and Oklahoma hometown earned him his nickname: the Commerce Comet.

Bonds won an all-time record seven MVP awards.

TODAY'S BIG BOPPER

One of the biggest home-run hitters of today is Phillies first baseman Ryan Howard. The big lefty swinger has at least 40 homers in four straight seasons. He set his career high in 2006 when he smacked 58 on his way to winning the N.L. MVP award. Howard's power also helped the Phillies win the 2008 World Series.

Howard favors the "pants over the shoetops" look of many modern players.

THE NEW STANDARD

In 2001, Barry Bonds of the San Francisco Giants may have put the single-season record for home runs permanently out of reach. With this swing against the Dodgers, e hit his 73rd homer of the year, three more than Mark McGwire's record set in 1998. In 2007, Bonds also captured the career mark, ending with a career total of 762 to overtake Hank Aaron's old mark of 755.

Did you know?

FASCINATING FACTS

Ichiro Suzuki

In 2009, Seattle outfielder Ichiro Suzuki broke a record that had stood for 108 years. Suzuki recorded his ninth straight season with 200 or more hits, knocking "Wee" Willie Keeler out of the record books. Keeler got the last of his eight straight 200-hit seasons in 1901.

Joe DiMaggio's streak of hitting safely in 56 consecutive games began on May 15, 1941. Over the next two months, he had at least one base hit in every game in which he played. During that time, he batted .408 with 15 home runs and 55 runs batted in. The streak finally ended on July 17, 1941, against the Cleveland Indians. DiMaggio hit safely in the next 16 games, giving him a streak of 72 out of 73 games.

In 2009, Philadelphia second baseman Eric Bruntlett made the 15th unassisted triple play in baseball history. Even more amazing, Bruntlett's was just the second ever to end a game. The only unassisted triple play in World Series history came in 1920, when the Indians' Bill Wambsganss pulled it off against the Dodgers.

On April 29, 1986, Roger Clemens of the Boston Red Sox set a Major League record by striking out 20 batters in a nine-inning game. Without walking a single batter and only giving up three hits, he got the win as the Red Sox defeated the Seattle Mariners, 3-1, at Fenway Park. Clemens struck out 20 for a second time in September 1996.

Mario Mendoza was a slick-fielding but dreadfully weak-hitting shortstop for three teams. When his batting average fell to .198 as a regular with Seattle in 1979, teammates began referring to .200 as the "Mendoza Line." Soon, Major League players stopped saying that a player couldn't hit his weight; now an unsuccessful hitter had sunk "below the Mendoza Line."

Singing the song "Take Me Out To the Ball Game" is a tradition during the seventh-inning stretch. The song was written in 1908 by Jack Norworth and Albert von Tilzer. At the time, neither man had ever seen a baseball game!

Only 14 players in Major League history have won the Triple Crown, an honor given to a player who leads his league in home runs, RBI, and batting average during the same season. The last to do it was Carl Yastrzemski of the Boston Red Sox, in 1967. Two players won the Triple Crown twice: Rogers Hornsby of the St. Louis Cardinals (in 1922 and 1925) and Ted Williams of the Red Sox (in 1942 and 1947).

The longest home run on record was a 565-foot (172 m) clout hit at old Griffith Stadium on April 17, 1953. Mickey Mantle, a switch-hitter for the New York Yankees, was batting right-handed against left-handed pitcher Chuck Stobbs of the Washington Senators.

In 1997, Major League Baseball honored Jackie Robinson on the 50th anniversary of his debut as the first African-American big-league player in the 20th century. MLB ordered Robinson's number 42 retired by all 30 Major League teams.

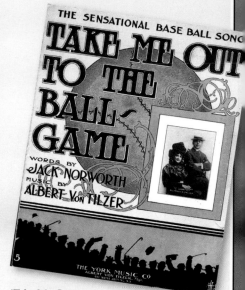

"Take Me Out to the Ball Game" song sheet

By joining the Seattle Mariners in 1990, Ken Griffey, Sr., made history. Ken Sr. and Ken Jr. became the first father and son to play in the Major Leagues as teammates. Then, on September 14, 1990, they hit back-to-back homers, another father-son first for Sr. and Jr.

A memorable All-Star Game moment occurred in 1934, when National League pitcher Carl Hubbell of the New York Giants struck out five future Hall of Famers in a row: Babe Ruth, Lou Gehrig, Jimmie Foxx, Al Simmons, and Joe Cronin. Hubbell himself was eventually inducted into the Hall of Fame.

The Detroit Tigers honored Jackie Robinson in 2009 by all wearing number 42.

QUESTIONS AND ANSWERS

Q Which two players together hold the all-time record for home runs by a pair of brothers?

A It's kind of a trick question: The answer is 768. Hank Aaron had 755, while his brother Tommie had 13!

Q When was the first pro baseball game aired on television?

A August 26, 1939. A doubleheader between Brooklyn and Cincinnati was shown on TV in New York City.

Q What was the last Major League ballpark to go without lights?

A Until 1988, Chicago's Wrigley Field did not have lights. The Cubs played all their home games in the daytime. Even with lights installed, they play the majority of their games in daylight.

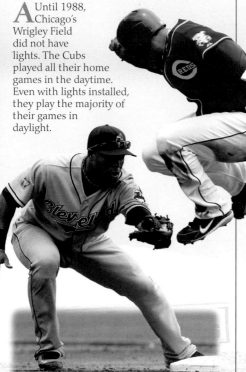

A base runner tries to avoid the fielder's tag.

Q Which little-known record did Seattle's Ichiro Suzuki break in 2004?

A On his way to an total of 262 hits, Ichiro smacked 225 singles, topping the old mark of 203 set by Willie Keeler (1898).

Q The batter hits a long fly ball that bounces on the field in fair territory and then lands untouched over the fence or into the stands. What is the umpire's call?

A Ground-rule double. The batter must stop at second base. A ground-rule double can also be called if a fan reaches out to touch a ball that is in play.

Q Who are the Bronx Bombers, the Halos, the Pale Hose, and the Friars?

A Those are nicknames for the New York Yankees, Los Angeles Angels, Chicago White Sox, and San Diego Padres, respectively.

Q Who were Big Poison and Little Poison, Dizzy and Daffy, and Tony C and Billy C?

A Those are nicknames for three pairs of baseball brothers: Paul and Lloyd Waner; Jay and Paul Dean; and Tony and Billy Conigliaro.

Q A fielder with the ball in his possession tags a runner leading off second base while the pitcher is not on the mound. What is the umpire's call?

A The runner is out. This is often called the "hidden-ball trick"; it is only legal when the pitcher is not on the mound.

Q What is a "can of corn"?

A An easy fly ball. The term comes from when old-time grocers used their aprons to catch cans knocked from a high shelf.

Perfect-game pitcher Mark Buehrle

Q What is a perfect game?

A This rare feat occurs when a starting pitcher wins the game without allowing a single player from the opposing team to reach a base. In 2009, Mark Buehrle became only the 18th pitcher to throw one.

Q What is the Hank Aaron Award?

A First given in 1999, this award goes to the best hitter, statistically, in each league. It is named for baseball's former all-time home-run king Hank Aaron, who is also the all-time leader in career RBI.

Q Who threw the first no-hitter?

A George Washington Bradley tossed the first one for the St. Louis Brown Stockings in 1876.

Baseball Math

Batting average

A player's batting average is equal to the number of hits divided by the number of at-bats. Example: A batter with 7 hits in 21 at-bats has a .333 batting average; this is calculated as 7 (hits) divided by 21 (at-bats). You can use the same formula to figure out a player's career or season average. A player with an average above .300 is considered a high-quality hitter.

Earned-run average (ERA)

ERA is the average number of earned runs a pitcher allows in a nine-inning game. It is calculated as the earned runs multiplied by nine and then divided by the number of innings pitched. Example: A pitcher who allows 10 earned runs in 30 innings pitched has an ERA of 3.00. This is calculated as 10 (earned runs) times 9 (innings per game), divided by 30 (innings pitched).

On-base percentage

A batter's on-base percentage is the number of hits plus walks plus times hit by a pitch, divided by the number of official at-bats plus walks plus times hit by a pitch plus sacrifice flies. Example: A batter with five hits and one walk in 11 official at-bats has a .500 on-base percentage (five hits plus one walk, divided by 11 at-bats plus one walk).

Slugging percentage

This is calculated by dividing the total number of bases a player has reached on singles, doubles (the number of doubles times two), triples (the number of triples times three), and home runs (the number of home runs times four) by his number of times at-bat. Example: A player with one home run and one double in 10 at-bats has six total bases in 10 at-bats for a .600 slugging percentage.

Baseball calendar

MAJOR LEAGUE BASEBALL's regular season goes from April through October. But baseball has become a year-round game. Here are some events to watch for during the year.

FEBRUARY AND MARCH
Spring Training. Pitchers and catchers report first, about two weeks before the position players. Teams training in Florida make up what is called the "Grapefruit League." Teams training in Arizona play in the "Cactus League."

APRIL
Opening Day. Celebrations take place in stadiums throughout both leagues. The highlight is the ceremonial first pitch, often thrown by a celebrity or politician, such as the president of the United States.

Jackie Robinson Day. On April 15, celebrations take place in stadiums throughout both leagues to honor Brooklyn Dodgers Hall of Famer Jackie Robinson. On this day in 1947, he became the first African-American ro play in the Major Leagues in the 20th century.

JUNE
College World Series. College teams from around the nation compete in Omaha, Nebraska, at Rosenblatt Stadium, host of the College World Series since 1950.

First-Year Player Draft. The Major League Baseball draft of high-school and college players is held by conference call among the 30 Major League clubs. Teams select in reverse order of winning percentage, regardless of league.

JULY
All-Star Game. The best players in the National and American Leagues compete in this game, held every year since 1933. The starting players are chosen by fans, who vote using official ballots. Some of the pitchers and substitutes are chosen by the managers of the two teams that played in the World Series the previous year, while others are chosen by players and fans. The winners get home-field advantage for their league in the World Series.

Hall Of Fame Induction Ceremony. Players become eligible for the Hall five years after they retire from playing. New members of the Hall are voted on by members of the Baseball Writers Association of America.

Trading Deadline. From the end of the season until August, Major League teams can trade players to help build their lineups. Starting in August, however, players need to clear waivers before they can be traded. A player on waivers can be claimed by any other team, which must purchase that player's contract.

AUGUST
Little League World Series. Teams from all over the world compete in this tournament, held near Williamsport, Pennsylvania, each summer since 1947. The final game is broadcast on national television. Little League has many age divisions, but this World Series is for the top teams of 11 to 13 year olds. Both boys and girls can play Little League at most levels.

SEPTEMBER
Major League rosters expand from 25 players to 40, giving numerous minor leaguers their first taste of the big leagues.

OCTOBER
The regular season ends near the beginning of the month, and the postseason begins.

Division Series: The three first-place teams and one wild-card team from each league face off in the Division Series. The League Championship Series (LCS) are played between the Division Series winners.

World Series: Since 1903, this series has determined the Major League Baseball champion. The LCS winners play in a best-of-seven series. The format usually has the two league champions meet for two games in the "home" city

All-Stars meet: Albert Pujols of the N.L. meets Derek Jeter of the A.L.

(see All-Star Game, above), then three games in the other city, returning for two more in the home city, if necessary.

NOVEMBER
Post-season Awards. After each season, members of the Baseball Writers Association of America vote for the players and pitchers they feel were the best in each league. The major awards are Most Valuable Player, Rookie of the Year, the Cy Young Award, Manager of the Year, and the Gold Gloves, given for fielding excellence.

DECEMBER
Winter Meetings. This is an annual conference when owners, team executives, and player representatives meet to discuss the state of the game and possible rule changes. Many blockbuster trades also occur during these meetings, which are held in a different city each year. Then it's just several long weeks until Spring Training starts again!

Preparations for the 2009 College World Series in Omaha, Nebraska

Baseball's all-time greats

THE HISTORY OF BASEBALL is filled with famous names, home-run heroes, pitching aces, and World Series–winning managers. You've met some of them in the pages of this book, but here's a subjective look at some top candidates for the best all-time at each position. This ranking takes into account offense, defense, championships, and impact on the game. Is your favorite player on here? If he's not, who do you think he should replace? That's one of the best things about talking baseball: There aren't really any "right" answers!

Babe Ruth's glove

CATCHER
Johnny Bench. Combine revolutionary defense (perfecting the one-handed catching technique) with powerful hitting (three N.L. RBI titles) and you've got the best overall catcher ever.
Josh Gibson. Although he never got his chance to play in the Major Leagues, Negro League star Gibson remains a legend for his stunning power at the plate. The stories say he had a tremendous throwing arm as well.

FIRST BASE
Lou Gehrig. The "Iron Horse" played in 2,130 consecutive games, while also putting up stunning numbers and winning the 1934 Triple Crown. The courage he displayed in facing the illness that took his life at the age of 37 remains a lesson for us all.
Albert Pujols. One of only two current players on this list, Pujols has finished in the top four in the MVP voting in eight of his nine seasons (winning three times), while topping 100 RBI each season.

SECOND BASE
Rogers Hornsby. Perhaps the best right-handed hitter of the 20th century, Hornsby won two Triple Crowns, seven N.L. batting titles, and his .424 mark in 1924 is still the highest since 1901.
Joe Morgan. Morgan's greatest skills were shown on the base paths—he stole 689 bags—and in the clubhouse. The quiet leader of the Big Red Machine was the MVP twice on two of the best teams of all time.

Rogers Hornsby

THIRD BASE
Mike Schmidt. Schmidt is probably the easiest choice on this list. He made it easy by slamming 548 homers while also winning 10 Gold Gloves for the Phillies along with three MVP awards.
Alex Rodriguez. Though he will be dogged by his early-career use of performance-enhancing drugs, A-Rod's skills showed through as he earned three MVP awards while making it to 500 homers in record time.

SHORTSTOP
Honus Wagner. Although he played more than a century ago, Wagner remains the best all-round shortstop ever, with blazing speed, tenacious defense, and eight N.L. batting titles.
Ozzie Smith. "The Wizard of Oz" is the only player on this list who made it on almost pure defense. His quickness, inventiveness, and agility led to game-changing glove work.

Albert Pujols

OUTFIELD
Hank Aaron. The 755 homers hit by "Hammerin' Hank" were the standard for three decades, while his courage in the face of racism as he chased the Babe inspired millions.
Barry Bonds. Both immensely talented and immensely controversial, Bonds has the single-season (73 in 2001) and career (762) homer records, but his legacy may be marred by allegations of drug use.
Ty Cobb. Ty Cobb was the best all-round ballplayer in the 20th century's first few decades, combining hitting skill (all-time best .366 average) with speed and grit.
Willie Mays. The "Say-Hey Kid" boasted power (660 homers), speed (four N.L. stolen base titles), and unmatched defense. Was he the best outfielder ever? Some say yes.

Babe Ruth. Without Ruth's stunning bat and outsized personality, would baseball be the game it is today? His home-run power rescued the game from the Black Sox Scandal, while his record-setting pitching with Boston makes him the hands-down best player ever.
Ted Williams. No one devoted himself to hitting more than "Teddy Ballgame," whose career .344 average is in the top 10 all-time and whose .406 mark in 1941 hasn't been topped since.

STARTING PITCHERS
Roger Clemens. "The Rocket" set an unreachable standard with seven Cy Young Awards, but post-career allegations of steroid use may have tarnished his stature.
Bob Gibson. How good was Gibson in 1968? His 1.12 ERA was the lowest in 54 years, and led the Major Leagues to lower the mound!
Walter Johnson. "The Big Train" boasted a nearly unhittable fastball, helping him set an all-time record with 110 shutouts and 417 total wins, second-most all-time.
Sandy Koufax. The best left-handed pitcher ever, Koufax had a five-year streak in the early 1960s that cemented his reputation, winning three Cy Youngs, throwing four no-hitters, and posting four seasons with ERAs under 2.05.
Christy Mathewson. While carving a place for college players in the early pros, Mathewson won 373 games, had five seasons of sub-2.00 ERAs, and earned a reputation as one of the game's true gentlemen.

RELIEF PITCHERS
Dennis Eckersley. Eck began as a starter, but moved to the bullpen in his 13th season. Soon, the sidearmer became an unhittable closer, with seven seasons of 33-plus saves.
Mariano Rivera. No pitcher in baseball history has been more effective in the big games, especially in the postseason, than this native of Panama. He's 8-1 with 39 saves and a tiny 0.74 ERA in playoff baseball.

MANAGERS
Connie Mack. Stick around to manage 50 years and you get this honor. The winningest—and losingest—skipper ever, he owned the teams that won five World Series.
Casey Stengel. Sure, he had the talent of the 1950s New York Yankees, but Stengel was the glue that tied them together well enough to win seven World Series and 10 A.L. pennants.

Find out more

BEING A BASEBALL FAN can be a big commitment, but it's also a lot of fun! There are all kinds of ways to get involved with the sport and learn more about your favorite players and teams. Whether you're visiting websites, collecting autographs, or watching a Major League game, it's easy to make baseball a part of your life all year round.

Bring your own pen to get autographs.

VISIT THE HALL OF FAME
The highlight of every trip to the Baseball Hall of Fame in Cooperstown, New York, is a visit to the hall of plaques honoring the members of the Hall, such as Red Sox great Ted Williams, above. New plaques are put up each summer following induction ceremonies attended by tens of thousands of fans. You can also check out thousands of pieces of famous gear, including bats, balls, gloves, pennants, tickets, and more.

SIGN MY BALL, PLEASE!
When you get to meet a real big-league star in person (like these folks who are meeting Phillies pitcher Cole Hamels), ask politely for an autograph. Make sure to have a pen and something to sign and be patient and polite. The only times on game days that players may be able to sign in person is before the game, usually after they have completed batting practice. This can be as much as two hours before a game. Call ahead to find out when the entry gates are opened before games at your ballpark.

USEFUL WEBSITES

www.mlb.com
The official website of Major League Baseball is packed with information about all the teams and players. Complete season and career stats can be checked, along with historical stats of thousands of former players. In addition, you can watch videos, listen to games, order gear, and check out the excellent World Series history section.

www.baseballhalloffame.org
Read about all the members of the Baseball Hall of Fame on this official site, which also includes photos of hundreds of pieces of historic memorabilia and a history of baseball uniforms.

www.littleleague.org
Find out where to play in your area and read about the Little League World Series. There are leagues for boys and girls of many ages.

www.espn.com/mlb
This site from one of MLB's official cable-television partners features in-depth scouting reports by reporters and analysts and articles by top national baseball writers.

BASEBALL IN THE MOVIES
Take us out to the ballpark . . . and the movie theater! Baseball and the movies have made for a winning team since the early days of both. The drama of the game, plus the comedy of the ballpark, have made for some of Hollywood's most memorable films. Plus, stars from Babe Ruth and Lou Gehrig to Steve Yeager and Keith Hernandez have appeared as themselves in movies. Many of the most memorable kid-friendly baseball movies mix baseball with a bit of fantasy. In *Little Big League*, a boy takes over as the manager of the Minnesota Twins. In *Rookie of the Year*, a freak accident gives another boy the greatest pitching arm in the world, which he uses to help his heroes on the Chicago Cubs. And in *The Sandlot* (above) a group of kids has to retrieve a priceless autographed baseball from the jaws of an angry neighborhood dog.

NATIONAL BASEBALL HALL OF FAME AND LIBRARY, COOPERSTOWN, NY
This shrine to baseball's past includes thousands of one-of-a-kind artifacts from heroes past and present. The highlight is the room where the more than 200 Hall of Fame members' plaques are displayed. A theater shows baseball movies, plus it's not unusual to have a chance to meet visiting former players.

NEGRO LEAGUES BASEBALL MUSEUM, KANSAS CITY, MO
Learn more about this important part of baseball history at this fascinating museum. Read about great players, see the gear they used, and watch special video presentations.

YANKEE STADIUM, NEW YORK, NY
The new home of the New York Yankees opened in 2009 as the largest stadium in the Majors. Fans visiting the stadium should make sure to visit Monument Park, located behind center field, which honors heroes from the Yankees' illustrious past.

FENWAY PARK, BOSTON, MA
The home of the Boston Red Sox is a treat for fans of any team. The oldest park still in use in the Majors, Fenway features an enormous left-field wall known as "the Green Monster." The park's location right in the middle of the busy city of Boston gives it a touch of old-time baseball flair.

WRIGLEY FIELD, CHICAGO, IL
The Chicago Cubs' home features real ivy growing on its famous brick outfield walls. While you're there, make sure to check out the seats on the roofs of the buildings outside the park.

CAUTION: KIDS HAVING FUN
Little League Baseball is the oldest and largest international youth baseball organization. Founded in 1939 in Pennsylvania, it now has teams in more than 100 countries. The children here, from Chula Vista, California, have just won the 2009 Little League World Series championship. Whether in Little League or some other youth baseball group, it's always rewarding to join up and "play ball." Ask your parents to check with your local parks and recreation department or check the Internet for baseball leagues in your area. You can also find baseball schools where you can practice your skills. A trip to a batting cage is a fun way to work on hitting, too.

GO TO THE BALLPARK!
Whether you go to a Major League park, a minor league park, a college game, a high-school game, or even a youth baseball game, there's nothing like watching baseball in person. The smell of the grass, the crack (or ping) of the bat, the sound of the ball falling into leather gloves—it's a huge part of summer for millions. At right, fans in Boston's Fenway Park watch from seats atop the park's famous left-field wall, known as the "Green Monster." But no matter where you sit at a ball game, you'll get an up-close view of some of the best sports action in the world.

Glossary

ASSIST Statistic credited to fielders when they throw runners out

BACKSTOP A high fence behind home plate that protects spectators and keeps batted or thrown balls within the field of play; also a slang term for the catcher

BALK If a pitcher tries to deceive a base runner after placing his foot on the pitcher's rubber, the umpire will call a balk; all runners advance one base.

BALL Any pitch outside the strike zone at which a batter does not swing

BASE RUNNER A player who safely reaches a base

BATTER An offensive player who comes up to home plate to try to get on base

BATTER'S BOX The six-foot by four-foot (1.8 by 1.2 m) rectangle on each side of home plate in which batters must stand when hitting

BULLPEN The area where pitchers warm up before and during games; usually located behind the outfield wall

BUNT A soft hit resulting from the batter holding the bat out and letting the ball hit it instead of swinging the bat. A batter will sometimes give himself up to advance a base runner.

CATCHER A defensive player who plays behind home plate and receives pitches from the pitcher

Chase Utley stands in as a batter.

CENTER FIELDER A defensive player who is positioned in the center of the outfield

CHANGE-UP A slow pitch that is usually thrown after several fast ones to throw off a batter's timing. A pitcher who throws a successful change-up is said to "pull the string."

COMPLETE GAME A game in which the same pitcher pitches every inning

CURVEBALL A pitch that curves as it reaches the plate. It is thrown by snapping the wrist sharply away from the body as the pitch is released, so the ball spins rapidly and veers to the left (if thrown with the right hand) or right (if thrown with the left hand).

Curveball grip

DIAMOND Another word for the infield

DOUBLE A hit on which the batter reaches second base safely.

DOUBLEHEADER When the same two teams play two games on the same date; also called a twin bill

Home plate

DOUBLE PLAY When two outs are made by the defense during one play; known by the offense as a "twin killing"; by the defense as the "pitcher's best friend"

DOUBLE STEAL A play in which two runners attempt to steal bases at the same time

EARNED RUN A run scored because of a hit, hit batter, or walk that is charged to a pitcher's earned run average (ERA). Runs that score because of errors are unearned.

EARNED RUN AVERAGE (ERA) The average number of earned runs a pitcher allows in a nine-inning game. It is calculated as a pitcher's earned runs allowed multiplied by nine and then divided by the number of innings pitched. Example: A pitcher who allows 10 earned runs in 30 innings pitched has an ERA of 3.00.

ERROR A misplay by a fielder that allows a runner to reach base safely or advance one or more bases; also called a bobble or a muff

FAIR TERRITORY Any part of the playing field within the foul lines

FASTBALL A straight pitch that is thrown with maximum speed and power. A fastball pitcher with a great "heater" is said to be "throwing smoke." Also called "high cheese."

FIRST BASEMAN A defensive player who is positioned on the right side of the infield near first base; also called the first sacker

FLY BALL A ball hit high in the air. A short fly ball also is called a pop-up. The term comes from the ball "flying" through the air.

FORCE PLAY A play in which the base runner must try to advance to the next base on a batted ball. In a force play, a fielder with the ball may get an out by touching the base ahead of the runner instead of tagging him.

FOUL BALL A ball that is hit but lands outside the foul lines

FOUL TIP A ball that just grazes a player's bat as he swings, and is then caught by the catcher

GRAND SLAM A home run with the bases loaded; also called a grand salami (slang)

GROUND BALL A ball that rolls or bounces on the ground; also called a grass cutter, grounder, or a worm burner (slang)

GROUND-RULE DOUBLE A play in which a batter is awarded two bases on a hit that lands in fair territory and then bounces over the fence or is interfered with by fans

HOME PLATE A rubber slab at which the batter stands to receive pitches. A batter must start and end a trip around the bases at home plate. Also called the dish (slang).

HOME RUN A four-base hit on which the batter scores a run for his team. A ball traveling over the fence is also called a four-bagger, round-tripper, fence-clearer, dinger, tater, jack, belt, long ball, bomb, moon shot, rain maker, clout, big bash, big fly, big swat, wallop, slam, or smash.

INFIELD The part of the field close to home plate that contains the bases; also called a diamond

INNING A segment of a baseball game in which each team has a turn at bat. Major League games (along with minor league and college games) are nine innings, while most youth baseball games are six innings.

LEFT FIELDER A defensive player who is positioned on the left side of the outfield

Catcher's mitt

MITT Another term for a fielder's glove, especially those worn by first basemen (whose mitts have elongated webbing) or catchers (whose mitts have extra padding)

NO-HITTER A game in which a pitcher or pitchers on the same team do not allow a base hit

ON-BASE PERCENTAGE A batter's total number of hits plus walks plus times hit by a pitch, divided by the number of at-bats plus walks plus times hit by a pitch plus sacrifice flies

OUTFIELD The large, grassy area beyond the infield

PASSED BALL A play in which a catcher fails to stop a pitch he should have caught, allowing a base runner to advance. If a passed ball comes on a third strike, the batter can run to first.

PEPPER A pregame exercise in which one player hits brisk grounders and line drives to a group of fielders who are standing about 20 feet (6 m) away. The fielders try to catch the ball and throw it back as quickly as possible. The batter hits the return throw.

PERFECT GAME A game in which a pitcher pitches every inning and does not let a runner reach base

PITCH A throw by the pitcher to a batter

PITCHER A defensive player whose job is to throw the baseball across home plate in an attempt to get the batter out. Pitchers stand on the mound at the center of the infield. They use a variety of types of throws when pitching.

PUTOUT A fielder is credited with a putout for catching a fly ball, pop-up, line drive, or throw that gets an opposing player out. A catcher receives a putout for catching a strikeout.

RIGHT FIELDER A defensive player who is positioned on the right side of the outfield

ROOKIE A player in his first season

RUNDOWN A play in which a base runner is trapped by the defense while between two bases, being chased back and forth, before either being put out or reaching a base safely

Chad Billingsley, Dodgers pitcher

SACRIFICE BUNT A sacrifice bunt allows a runner to advance to another base at the expense of the batter, who is out. A sacrifice fly is a fly ball which is caught by a fielder, but which allows a runner to then tag up and score.

SAVE A pitcher gets credit for a save by finishing a close game while protecting his team's lead. If his team has a big lead, he can get a save by pitching the last three innings.

SCREWBALL A pitch that usually curves toward the left when thrown by a left-handed pitcher, and toward the right when thrown by a right-handed pitcher.

SECOND BASEMAN A defensive player who is positioned on the right side of the infield between first base and second base

SHORTSTOP A defensive player who is positioned on the left side of the infield between second base and third base

SHUTOUT A game completed by a pitcher without allowing a run to the opposition. The term can also refer to any game in which a team loses without scoring any points.

SINGLE A one-base hit; also called a base knock or bingle

SLIDER A pitch that is gripped more loosely than a curveball so that the ball "slides" out of the pitcher's hand. It looks like a fastball but curves sharply just as it reaches the plate.

SPIKES Nickname for baseball shoes, which usually have metal studs or other projections to help players dig into the dirt

SQUEEZE PLAY A play that starts with a bunt and often leads to a run. With a runner on third, the batter drops down a bunt, and the runner charges toward home plate, trying to reach it before the catcher or another fielder can retrieve the ball.

STOLEN BASE A base gained by advancing when a batter does not hit a pitch

STRIKE Any pitch that passes through the strike zone or at which a batter swings and misses. An uncaught foul ball with fewer than two strikes also counts as a strike, as does a fouled bunt attempt (even with two strikes) and a foul tip (with two strikes, it must be caught cleanly by the catcher to result in a third strike).

STRIKEOUT An out recorded when a pitcher delivers three strikes (including foul balls) to a batter during an at-bat

STRIKE ZONE The area over the plate from the batter's knees up to the midpoint between the top of his uniform pants and shoulders. If a pitch passes through this area and the batter doesn't swing, the umpire calls a strike.

TAG To touch a player with the ball for an out. The ball can be in the fielder's hand or held inside his glove.

TAGGING UP Returning to touch base after a fly ball is caught for an out. Base runners must wait until the ball has been caught before leaving a base to advance to the next open base or to score.

Michael Bourn lays down a squeeze bunt.

THIRD BASEMAN A defensive player who is positioned on the left side of the infield near third base. This area is known as the "hot corner."

TRIPLE A three-base hit; also known as a three-bagger

WALK A free trip to first base, awarded to a batter after a pitcher has issued four balls during one at-bat. A walk is symbolized by the letters BB in scoring, for "base on balls."

WALK-OFF HIT A hit that results in the winning run being scored in the bottom of an inning, leading to the instant end of the game

Strike zone

Index

Acknowledgments

The author, the publisher, and the Shoreline Publishing Group would like to thank the following for their assistance in creating this book: John Horne of the National Baseball Hall of Fame and Library; David Spindel and his marvelous memorabilia collection; Bryan Emrich of Wilson/DeMarini/ATEC for supplying photos of their baseball gear; and Eric Enders and Jim Gigliotti for their baseball eagle-eyes. Special thanks to Bill Pintard and the national-champion Santa Barbara Foresters, including players/models Adam Berry and Wade Clark.

The following books and websites were resources for the author. Note that all statistics are current through the end of the 2009 season.

Books:
Total Baseball (Sport Classic Books, 2004) by John Thorn et al.

The Dickson Baseball Dictionary, Third Edition (W.W. Norton, 2009) by Paul Dickson
Green Cathedrals (Addison Wesley, 1992) by Philip J. Lowry
The Series (Sporting News, 1991)

Websites:
www.mlb.com
www.baseball-reference.com
www.si.com
www.sportingnews.com

Photography Credits:
t = top; b = bottom; l = left;
r = right; c = center

Courtesy of Amherst College Archives and Special Collections, photo by Samuel Manister: 46cl
AP/Wide World: 10bc, 11l, 11tc, 11br, 11cr, 13tc, 15tr, 20c, 22bl, 23l, 23cr, 25cr, 26br, 28cl, 29tr, 29br, 30br, 31tr, 32b, 33tl, 34br, 36br,

37cr, 37br, 41tl, 41cr, 42bl, 42br, 42r, 43tr, 43c, 43br, 46cr, 47cr, 47b, 48tr, 49tr, 50cl, 50r, 51tr, 53br, 55b, 56cl, 56cr, 56t, 57l, 57cr, 57br, 59tr, 60cl, 60c, 60bl, 60tr, 61l, 61cr, 62r, 62l, 63tr, 63l, 64b, 65tr, 66b, 66t, 67bl, 68r, 69tl
Michael Burr: 16c, 16b, 17br, 17c, 21l, 23br, 24l, 25t, 27l, 27cr, 30c, 36cr, 40tl, 49bl, 58bc, 59bc, 60cr, 70bl
Corbis: 68br
Mike Eliason: 14tl, 14c, 17bl, 18c, 20l, 21br, 24r, 25bc, 26cl, 31br, 48cl, 49cr, 59br
Focus on Baseball: 12l, 12t, 13tr, 13c, 13br, 15tl, 19br, 24bl, 28t, 28c, 30bc, 31l, 32tr, 33cl, 33cb, 33b, 34bl, 34tr, 35tl, 35br, 36bl, 37l, 37tr, 47tl, 48cr, 52bl, 52br, 53tl, 53cr, 63br, 64tl, 65l, 64-65 background, 66-67 background, 67c, 68tl, 68-69 background, 69br, 70tl, 70-71 background, 71l, 71tr
Getty Images (photographers listed): AFP: 43tl; Jim Baird/Union-Tribune: 12c; Collegiate Images: 46b (3), 47tr; Tom DiPace/SI: 57tr; Jed Jacobsohn: 59l, 61tr; Chuck Solomon/SI: 56bl, 56br; Jamie Squire: 35tc
Library of Congress: 18tl
National Baseball Hall of Fame and Library: 6c, 6b, 7t, 8tl, 8br, 9t, 9bl, 10tl, 11cr, 14tr, 17tr, 21tr, 22cr, 23tr, 25cl, 25c, 26bl, 27br, 30bl, 33tr, 34tl, 36tl, 39tl, 40tl, 40tr, 41c, 40bl (2),

45l, 45br, 45tl, 46tr, 47tl, 50tl, 51cl, 51tc, 54bl, 54br, 55t (5), 58tl, 64r
David Spindel: 6l, 7r, 7b, 8bl, 8c, 8cr, 9tr, 9br, 10bl, 10r, 11tr, 18cl, 18bl, 20r, 21bl, 22tr, 22br, 26tl, 26cr, 26br, 30tr, 32tl, 36cl, 38cl, 38bl, 39cl, 40br, 52t (4), 53tr, 58bl, 58cr, 58br, 58tr, 59bl, 62c, 63tl
Shoreline Publishing Group: 6r, 48b
Slap Shot Photography: 40b, 41bc
Transcendental Graphics: 38tr, 67tr
University of Notre Dame Libraries: 51tl, 51b
Courtesy Wilson/DeMarini/ATEC: 18br, 19c, 19r (3), 27r, 31bc, 46tl, 70br

Jacket images: Front: Kyle Alexander/Brand X Pictures/JupiterImages (b), Transcendental Graphics, Michael Burr (tcl), National Baseball Hall of Fame and Library (tc, bcl), David Spindel (bc, tcr, r). Back: Michael Burr (l, tr, bc), David Spindel (tc), Courtesy Wilson/DeMarini/ATEC (cr, r), National Baseball Hall of Fame and Library (br).